Speaking
with Ease

Handy Tips & Highly Practical Examples for Public & Employment-Related Presentations

Crystal Rae Coel Coleman, M.A., J.D.

KENDALL/HUNT PUBLISHING COMPANY
4050 Westmark Drive   Dubuque, Iowa 52002

Cover images:
Photo of Darrell Young speaking; photo by Amber B. DuVentre.
Photo of speaking at a business meeting © 2009 by JupiterImages Corporation.
Photo of woman at podium © 2009 by JupiterImages Corporation.

Contents

*Each presentation has tips and a sample manuscript
or a sample manuscript outline.*

(An asterisk indicates presentations with impromptu elements, which
often have question and answer forums during or after the presentation.)

CHAPTER 8   **A Quick Impromptu Guide**

The Four Part Structure

Foreword

Before we ask children to walk or even to eat solid foods, we ask them to say words like "mama" and "dada." Other than teaching them new words and correcting pronunciation, we do very little to help them learn how to communicate effectively with others. All students leave high school having had the opportunity to learn reading, writing, and arithmetic (among other subjects), but rarely do they actually learn effective communication concepts and skills.

The same is true in the business world. There is an expectation that employees can communicate effectively, but organizations rarely want to invest the time or money to enhance someone's competency with what we call a "soft skill." When businesses consider where to spend the few resources allotted for an individual's development, they do not often spend them on presentation courses or materials. Financial resources are limited, and the return on a business investment is paramount. Some companies believe that learning new accounting software is more important than learning communication skills. However, many are now recognizing the importance of outstanding presentation skills. Sales increase when a presenter is an excellent persuasive or informative speaker. Therefore, businesses have made a greater effort to hire consultants to help employees improve communication competencies, ranging from learning to listen better to creating better public and employment-related presentations. The reality is that no person gets anywhere in this world without an ability to express desires and concerns.

I don't think I understood the importance of public address when I took my first communication class at the age of thirteen. However, I knew that speech, creativity, and organization attracted me. After my first day in a college forensics class, I knew I had found my passion, which eventually led to multiple careers as a communication instructor, forensics coach, and corporate consultant. However, it was not until my first teaching job that I actually read through an entire public speaking textbook. If you have ever looked through any guide for effective public speaking, you know why it took me so long to actually read the massive amount of information given for a sixteen-week college course. Theory and course specific jargon are important; but, really, who has time for all that information in such a short period of time? Readers don't retain most material, especially students who feel "forced" to take introductory speech classes. People who are out of school and into their careers want quick reference guides like this text. This text is practical to have for a classroom, for an organization, or for a bookshelf in your house.

Whether it was my time as a public speaking instructor and debate coach at Clemson University or my job as a facilitator of leadership development for Tyson Foods, Inc., the one thing that never changed was the need to help people communicate more effectively. The other constant has been the need to build these skills in people in a relatively short amount of time. In today's society, being first to market is a competitive advantage. Therefore, when you need to communicate quickly, with clarity, and credibility, you don't want to spend a lot of time preparing your presentation. It is refreshing to find a book that helps you to communicate effectively and that also saves you valuable time.

So whether you are in a speech class learning how to give your first persuasive keynote address, at a wedding delivering your best friend's toast, or at a business meeting making a formal proposal to the CEO of your company, we all need guidance with how to effectively express our thoughts to our audience. This book will help you accomplish your public speaking goals without forcing you to endure pages of theory. The time you will save, the expert advice and the sample manuscripts/outlines by Crystal Rae Coel Coleman, and the extra tips and examples from outstanding contributing writers will help you to grow both personally and professionally. This is one of those books that you will keep on your shelf as a handy reference throughout your career and your life. Don't start another presentation without first consulting this book!

Jennifer Haas, M.S.
Leadership and Executive Development Coach
Former Leadership Facilitator for Tyson Foods, Inc.

Preface

DON'T READ THIS ENTIRE BOOK!

I wrote a text under two hundred and fifty pages so that you wouldn't feel compelled to read a text with over four hundred and fifty pages only to realize you just needed the information from pages 14 through 19, 212 through 220 and 408 through 436 to complete most of your assignments. With this text, you can read key information from the first few chapters. Then, you can go directly to the presentation you need to give without trying to sift through jargon and long examples that complicate a process that a quick explanation and a brief example can simplify. All of the tips, manuscripts, and manuscript outlines are original work products. With the exception of a few quotations, everything was created and written just for this text.

I've taught introductory and advanced levels of public address for over twenty years. After using several recommended texts over and over, I have realized two key things: Many students only "scan" lengthy speech texts and they read only enough information to pass the exam; and many have told me that they don't even buy their expensive speech texts because after they hear the lecture about organizing a presentation, they realize the rest is about practicing the delivery. Therefore, I have written this text that offers a guide for public speaking along with practical examples of presentations, without the lengthy explanations and the expense of larger texts.

I've heard scholars go back and forth: large text, small text, or no text? However, one thing is clear: The students who enroll in public speaking courses and people in general, want things done quickly due to time constraints! Regardless of whether that is intellectually correct, I do believe that it does not compromise the integrity of the discipline to let people know how to construct a presentation by using simple concepts and techniques before revealing an example that triggers their own creativity.

This text is a handbook with quick references and complete brief examples. There are explanations and sample manuscripts or manuscript outlines for the lecture, report of research findings, introduction of a speaker, keynote address, press conference, debate, announcement, tour, sales pitch, team symposium, panel discussion, presentation and acceptance of an award or gift, religious service, eulogy, roast, wedding toast, and more!

Many people learn by reading a concrete example and then doing the assignment. I would certainly never criticize thorough preparation. As a matter of fact, I embrace the advanced study of presentational speaking. However, sometimes "less is more," especially with a discipline that creates so much anxiety. Students in my speech classes tell me that they learn and retain more by listening to my personal experiences as a professional speaker, reading a minimal amount of jargon, and seeing the word for word example that is realistic and outlined.

Many texts have speeches by famous people, and for many students, the language used or the structure set forth seems unattainable and overwhelming. Student speeches are better, but often the topics are generic and will do little to help students prepare for real-life applications. In addition, various people from an entrepreneur to a server have told me that they just don't have time to read some big college textbook or write a presentation for a last-minute meeting or event; so, they usually "throw something together" and hope it's decent. I want people to go from throwing something together, to quickly creating a quality presentation.

Of course, this handbook will not cover every aspect of public address. This handy text has short and easy to understand examples of presentations. Any adult can read this text and create a presentation for a college course, a work-related situation, or an organization's event without feeling as if he or she has to spend weeks putting it together. A theory-based text for advanced communication studies can explain the historical background, perspectives, and deep levels of rhetoric. This text is for something else.

This text is for:

- The professor/instructor who wants students to learn about presentations they may actually have to give one day

- The student who has many courses, activities, and work obligations but who also wants his or her education to be meaningful and not just "busy work"

- The profit and non-profit employers and employees who have to write several different types of presentations each year but never had just one core text as a reference for the diversity of presentations

- The stay at home and working moms and dads who belong to organizations where they have to prepare presentations for the multiple events and causes they champion

This handbook has several features:

- Handy tips from the author or other professionals in their respective fields

- Highly practical, full sentence manuscripts or manuscript outlines so the reader can read an actual presentation and not just read "how to do it"

- Descriptions of the presentations, including an audience profile, time constraints, possible locations, suggested aids, etc. that readers may find useful for preparing the final draft

- A chapter of informative *and* persuasive presentations that the Table of Contents alphabetizes for easy reference

- Explanations about impromptu situations as they apply to certain presentations (The Contents identifies presentations with impromptu elements with an asterisk.)

- A chapter guide for impromptu speaking that serves as a quick reference if you are asked to speak with no time to prepare, and there are some suggestions for the question and answer forum

- An index with cross-references

Acknowledgements

I first give thanks, praise, and humble acknowledgements to my God as the Father, the Son Jesus Christ and the Holy Spirit. He has taught me everything and has forgiven everything. He has strengthened me and He has humbled me. This was an experience that He allowed me to share with so many. God as the Trinity is my best friend.

I am grateful to have in my life: my loving husband Ronald Edward Coleman who supported me and said he was proud of me for writing this text; my dad Raphael M. Coel and my mother (posthumously) Julia Echols Coel, who both encouraged me, taught me that "impossible" is ridiculous, and who spent their lives trying to enrich mine. I love you. I am forever grateful. I thank my family members the: Brewingtons, Youngs, Echols, Randles, Harrells/Stiths/Hills, Thompsons, who reside in Maryland/Washington, D.C., Pennsylvania, Nevada, Michigan, Virginia, North Carolina, etc. for loving me. I love you too. I have so much love for my mother-in-law Irma Coleman who is a source of strength, my brother-in-law Steve, sister-in-law Joyce and Godmothers Helen McMurray, Idella Nichols, Ellen Echols, Adele Brown and Miss Ellen Dutton. I love the Danny/Wendy Ball, Eric Walker and Al Taylor families. God Bless you Uncle David.

I thank Kendall/Hunt, especially Senior Acquisitions Editor Terry Brennan who believed in my vision for this book and made me feel confident others would believe in it too; and Senior Project Coordinator Angela Puls who made me feel like I produced a quality product that could help others do what I love to do: TALK! (smiles) Dr. George Cullen, Dr. Patrick Hebert and Judge Louis Hill always encouraged me to embrace my love for speaking so I could create positive messages to share. Judge Eugene H. (posthumously) and Mrs. Annie Clarke are loved!

I thank the photographers and the contributing writers who created images, tips or quotes and who wrote manuscripts or outlines for the book. You are great friends and associates! In alphabetical order I thank you: Paul Wesley Alday, M.A., Dr. Andrew C. Billings, Valoria L. Cheek, Esquire., Jennifer R. Coleman, M.S., Lisa Corum, Dr. Catherine Cushinberry, Amber B. DuVentre, M.S., Agnes C. DuVentre, Jerry W. Drye, M.S., DeChelle L. Forbes, M.A., Kristen K. Gunderson, Jennifer Haas, M.S., Karen Hill Johnson, M.S., M.S., Maria E. Locklear, M.S., Emma L. Millman, Patty S. Parish, M.S., April Rene Payne, F. Trice Seargent III, Elana K. Thompson, David A. Yastremski, M.S.,

Pastor Darrell R. Young. I love you for being unselfish and for sharing your talents for this project. I could not have produced this product without you! You are so special! Todd M. Schultz, Mona Lisa Warren, Linda Pierce, Jessica Haynes! You rock!

To my friends at Calvary Temple and those in Philly at Greater Saint Matthew (G.S.M.I.C), thank you for your prayers. I also appreciate my colleagues at Murray State University: the Department of Organizational Communication and the College of Business and Public Affairs, the Black Faculty and Staff Association, the Council of College Heads and Dr. Robertson, Jenilee Crutcher Williams, Dawn Gupton, student workers Dustin L. Smith, Tyler Smith, Linzy Rollins, Sara Blandford, and Kristin Wilford. I thank Luke Finck, Kim Bridges, Meagan Drye, Dr. B. Koenecke, Dr. R. Weis, Tammy Elkins and Shad Young. Lori Evans, Kim Shea, Marc Gomez, Andrea Bailey, Stephanie Burkeen and the staff at Hickory Woods Retirement Center have been a blessing to my family. Also, Andrea Chapman, Jessica Weatherford, Ronald Wells, Robin Phelps, Allen Hendricks, Danielle Klein, Gabe Barrett, Troy Williams, the Duffy's, Webers, Cohoons, Buchs, Professors Robin Orvino, Bobbie Greer, Patricia Huber, Karen B. Allen and family and Dr. Mittie Nimocks are special. I thank Tallana LK and Brandon B. (posthumously), Jeanne P., Lisa L.S., Brian W., Dan W., Stephanie S.M., Sandy S., Ty W., Jeanne H.C. and Terry M. for the UWP memories. Thanks to my mentors within the American and National Forensic Associations (especially Dan, John, Richard, Frank, Gary and Leigh Ann, Bob, Billy, Kimberly, David, Judy, Karen, Kelly Jo, Judi, Larry and Mark) and my longtime friends on the East Coast: The Owen Wallace Family, Lori B. Clark, Charlene Wayns Williams (Katrina, Christine, Kevin C. and Cherie too), Adele D'Angelo Masters and the "crew" (Heather, Peggy, Barb, Kathy, Patty, JoAnne, Gretchen, etc.), the Hibblers, Johnsons, Starkmans, Kesslers, Koss's, and the DJ and Lisa Bryant family. Of course, I absolutely ADORE the gentle spirit, soft love, encouraging and calm presence when I needed a good friend . . . when things were hectic and exhausting . . . MK—Amazing . . . Precious . . . Special . . . Smiles (Tagger and Sabre) (Lu Lu and Puff—posthumously).

I love all of my students who have endured my classes. Someone once said, "What doesn't kill us, makes us stronger." I cherish my students of the Murray State Speech and Debate Union and those who are a part of Elizabeth College—(GO LIZO!). I have so much love for the class of 1985 at Hampton University. (GO PIRATES!) I thank God for having all of you in my life. I am very grateful . . . I am truly blessed!

About the Author

Author photo courtesy of Lisa Corum

Crystal Rae Coel (pronounced like Noel but with a "C") Coleman, M.A., J.D., (Esquire), is the Director of Speech and Debate in the Organizational Communication Department within the College of Business and Public Affairs. She's been at Murray State University for over fourteen years. She also enjoys serving as the Head of Elizabeth College. It is one of the eight residential colleges, with each one having over 1200 students, staff, and faculty members. She is Murray State's first African-American College Head.

Dr. Coleman has appeared in *Who's Who in Education* and *Who's Who in American Law.* Her expertise is in public address, debate, mediation, broadcast performance, team communication, and leadership. She's an active and licensed Pennsylvania attorney, a certified mediator, motivational speaker and corporate consultant. Her clients have included but are not limited to the National Weather Service, Kroger subsidiaries KenLake Foods, Inc. and Delight Products, Inc. and The American Baptist Extension Corporation. She is also one of the authors for the textbook *A Manner of Speaking.*

Coel Coleman is from suburban Philadelphia, PA (Haverford Township). She received her Bachelor of Arts in Mass Media and Journalism from Hampton University in Virginia, her Master of Arts in Communications with an emphasis in public address from the University of Louisiana at Monroe, and her Doctor of Jurisprudence from the Southern University Law Center. She has taught in London, England and at the University of Wisconsin at Platteville, the University of Louisiana at Monroe and the Community College of Philadelphia. She is a member of many academic honor societies and professional communication and legal organizations. Over the past 20 years, she has received numerous awards for forensics and teaching excellence. She has been a contributing writer/consultant for textbooks and her article *Campaign 2008: The Legal and Ethical Considerations of Rhetorical Posturing and Media Strategies* appears in the *Kentucky Journal of Communication.* She loves God as the Trinity, her husband, her family members, her friends and her students.

CHAPTER

1

Knowing Your People, Places, and Things

Too often people want to jump right in and start a presentation without considering three major questions: To whom am I speaking? What are the location and the time of the presentation? What are the things I must consider for the overall effectiveness of my presentation?

THE PEOPLE

There are several things to consider when it comes to your audience. You must know as much as you can about your audience *before* you try to pick a topic or write the presentation. The following are just a few core demographics to consider:

- Age
- Gender
- Economic class
- Race or cultural background
- Work or group affiliation
- Educational level

If you are not sure about the members of your audience:

- Ask the person who invited you to speak to tell you the audience demographics and what to expect

- Ask someone who has already been a speaker for that audience

- If the audience members belong to a specific organization, research that organization and its member affiliation

- If there is time and the audience is not too large, you can create a questionnaire and have the members fill it out a few weeks before the presentation and have them send it back to you. The questionnaire should be brief and contain a mixture of essay and multiple choice questions along with questions that require a "yes" or "no" response. This would require you to be organized and in contact with a person who has addresses of the attendees. Make sure you have permission to contact those who may attend.

THE PLACES (AND TIME)

Where Is the Presentation?

Before you attempt to write a speech, you must analyze the location. Ask yourself whether the presentation is:

- In a large city with diverse opinions and experiences or in a smaller town where many people share the same experiences and co-cultures

- In a different country with different values and expectations

- In a hotel, a church building, a civic center, etc.

- In a large room or in a small room

- In an area with a podium or a lectern or in an area without these things

- In a room with a hot, cold, or comfortable temperature

- In an area restricted by seating arrangements

If the setting is too comfortable or uncomfortable, you can lose your audience and they will tune you out. Notice the temperature, the pictures on the walls, and the seating arrangement. Make sure you do not stand with your back to anyone. If you are forced to speak with people seated behind you, you must constantly talk and then turn to acknowledge those behind you. This has only happened to me once. It was annoying but I did adjust to this unusual seating arrangement! Don't forget to make sure that everyone can hear you with or without a microphone. Also, if the location is uncomfortable, you may need to shorten the presentation.

Image © Monkey Business Images, 2009. Used under license from Shutterstock, Inc.

In the United States, large diverse audiences are usually more open to controversial topics. Research cultures and co-cultures and understand what language is acceptable and what language is offensive. Also, presentations for people from different countries can be tricky. In addition to your language usage, be aware of your nonverbal communication, as other countries do not accept some of our symbols in the United States.

When Is the Presentation?

Timing is not everything but it means a lot! There are three times to examine:

- Time limit for the presentation
- Time of year
- Time of day

The time limit you receive will affect whether you can have audience interaction, a question and answer period, and so forth. The time of day is crucial in determining the topic and style of delivery. The time of year can affect location comfort thus affecting your content and the length of the presentation.

- Make sure you ask for a time limit and adhere to that limit. You can be embarrassed if the host has to stop your presentation or ask you afterwards why it was so short after requesting that you speak a certain length of time.

- Most listeners are alert for presentations before 11 A.M.

- Presentations during or after lunch require a less technical topic and much more humor and/or animation for the delivery.

- Entertaining evening presentations are popular with mixed audiences and audiences that are highly motivated and energetic.

- Presentations during the winter or summer months require an awareness of potential weather discomfort. If it's too cold or too hot, audience members tune out the message—even if they don't want to. Be prepared to end the presentation early if you notice audience members are uncomfortable. Do not stop abruptly! You still need that summary and creative closure!

 THE THINGS

Why Am I Speaking?

There are two primary reasons why you have to give a presentation: to inform your audience about a topic or to persuade your audience about a topic. It does not matter what the occasion is; there are really only two purposes for presenting. Whether you want to be serious so others retain information or whether you want to entertain *in addition* to giving information, your presentation will be informative, persuasive, or both!

What Topic Is the Most Appropriate?

Appropriate stands for:

- A topic that will not overtly offend your diverse audience

- A topic that challenges and does not insult your audience's intellect

- A topic that will fit the time limits you have

- A topic that is interesting and will allow for vivid language that engages your audience

Brainstorm topics based on your personal background, family life, professional experiences, values, religious beliefs, political beliefs, recreational activities, and so forth. Once you have a list, start to narrow the list based on the five W's: who, what, when, where, and why. If you have to give a presentation with demonstration elements, then you would explore "how."

Kristin Wilford and Luke Finck discuss topic selection.

Remember to:

- Speak to the event theme if there is one and to the occasion

- Speak about something you have experienced, something you researched, or something you learned from listening to others

- Speak to the audience's interest

- Use language that does not assume gender roles; i.e. police*man*

Podium or Freestyle?

Knowing whether you will have a podium (or lectern) makes a huge difference in the style of delivery you choose. In the classroom, some students insist that they would rather speak without the podium. However, when they don't have one and cannot pace back and forth, the majority of students feel awkward. It's best to learn how to present with and without the podium. Some locations will not have a podium or a microphone. Without a podium, you must be more animated with your visual delivery and louder with your verbal delivery. However, you also have to be poised. You don't want to pace back and forth or wave your hands around too much or you will distract the audience and the message will get lost.

Technical Capabilities?

It's important to ask in advance if there are technical devices for you to use. If the room is large, you will need a microphone. The lavaliere microphones that attach to one's clothing are the best. They allow for the free movement of your hands and body. The handheld microphone is a second option that will allow you to move freely throughout the complex. However, it will become annoying if you wish to be active with your audience because you will have to keep putting it down and picking it up. This is why it's necessary to know the type of presentation. For workshops where walking around and monitoring teams is necessary, the lavaliere is best. Religious services or keynote addresses often utilize the handheld or podium microphones.

In addition to microphones, you may need additional audio or video equipment to enhance your message. Make sure you have practiced with all equipment before you get in front of your audience. You need to know if the location has the technical capabilities you need before you create your final draft. Too often, I've witnessed employees from major corporations fumble with equipment in front of the audience thus losing credibility. This won't happen if you investigate the technology available and the limitations before you even get to the location. If you bring your own devices, make sure they are compatible with the technology at the location. Check the screens, the sound, the visual elements, etc. Is everything large enough, clear enough, and loud enough? If possible, you should get to the site a day early or at least hours before you give the presentation. This way, you can rehearse and test everything!

Relaxing Your Mind

So many people fear public speaking. There is no "pill" you can take to conquer this fear. The best remedies for helping to reduce the anxiety are:

1. Reassuring yourself that you really can give a presentation
2. Understanding that people want to hear your information and they are not in the audience to judge you or to laugh at you
3. Realizing that the more knowledgeable you are about the subject and the more you rehearse, the less nervous you will be
4. Understanding that skill-building courses and materials will enhance your confidence level
5. Practice, practice, practice

Introducing
and
Concluding

 # In the financial world:

- You must intrigue your audience with your introduction and conclusion. In my career, I often present complex financial topics. The ability to identify with the audience's frames of reference and probable life experiences is the best way to capture their attention.

- A clever and concise introduction and conclusion are what my audience remembers. Even though I would like my audience to retain the majority of the information that I cover, it's not realistic. The most pressing issues on their minds when I give a presentation might be an end-of-the-month deadline or an upcoming vacation.

- In my career, I might present a retirement planning workshop for a group of thirty professionals, but very few will fully comprehend the details of retirement planning. If I can compel them to retain my introduction and conclusion, they will think of me when they are ready to absorb the details and apply them to their situations.

Kristen Gunderson
Relationship Manager
First Tennessee Bank
Nashville, TN

 # PURPOSE OF THE INTRODUCTION

If you start with confidence and competence, you and your audience will feel better about your ability to give an excellent presentation.

Most introductions should:

1st   Intrigue the audience

2nd   Introduce the topic and tell the audience why you're qualified to speak

3rd   Explain the benefit(s) of listening to the topic

4th   Preview two to five main points in one or two sentences

Presentations that are extremely short, like an "announcement" or a "toast," and those that are more dialogue-based, like a "press conference" or an "interview," may not require all of the elements of the introduction.

Ways to Intrigue the Audience (with or without Humor)

RHETORICAL OR DIRECT QUESTION OR SET OF QUESTIONS

You can ask questions rhetorically with no response needed:

- How many people love their best friend?

- Is everyone in this room ready for a good time?

- Do you want your child safe; do you want your child to live longer than you; do you want your child to be the best he or she can be?

Direct questions require a verbal or nonverbal response:

- How has divorce changed your life?

- Since all of you were caught cheating on exams, what motivated each one of you to cheat?

- Has anyone in this room tried to quit smoking?

SHORT PERSONAL STORY

When I was fifteen years old, my mother was diagnosed with cancer. One day she fainted, and we just thought she was tired. However, after several tests and trips to the hospital, they told us that she had this horrible disease. Back in the 1980s the word "cancer" meant an automatic death sentence. The family became so sad, and we prepared to lose her. We gathered her things, drafted the will, and prepared to lose our best friend. She told us what she wanted for our lives, but her doctors were wonderful, and prayer works. After several treatments, the cancer was gone, and we all celebrated a rebirth of my mother!

SHORT PUBLISHED STORY

She is sixteen years old. Her name is Susan. The perspiration of desperation glues her hair to the sides of her face. She walks the streets of Washington hoping for someone to notice her. Each day she is afraid of being killed and afraid of being rescued. She cannot imagine being happy. She only knows fear and sadness as she looks out her window. She looks at the city from her small apartment that she shares with two other girls who work for Rita. Rita is nice but Rita demands the best from "her girls." Susan is one of Rita's girls and one of America's thousands of lost children who could be found if they knew someone cared . . . This comes from the article "The Lost Children of This Country" from the September 30, 2008 issue of the *Hampton Children Magazine.*

(Fictitious magazine and citation)

EMOTIONAL STATEMENT

- Look at the person to your right; look at the person to your left; in ten years, one of you will be dead.

- There are twenty teenagers in this room, and ten of you have tried drugs.

EMOTIONAL ACTION

You can bang on a podium, throw something soft into the audience, and do a strange body movement . . . anything that startles or excites the audience. You can do anything that creates a strong emotion that makes the audience want to hear what you have to say.

QUOTATION WITH THE AUTHOR CITED

- My favorite teacher Cullen Hebert once said, "If you can't say something nice, you probably are miserable inside!" (Fictitious name and quote)

- Televangelist Ms. M once said during a conference, "When it comes to arguing with your husband, sometimes you have to let it go . . . after all, do you want to be right or do you want to be happy?" (Fictitious name and quote)

Reveal the Topic and Qualify Yourself

When you immediately inform your audience that you are speaking about a particular subject, it puts them in a position to actively listen. When the audience has to stretch their necks and tilt their heads in confusion, then the presenter is not audience-focused. The listeners should immediately know the subject area. One or two short sentences will suffice:

> *It is important that we go over the plans for the office picnic. As the chairperson for this event, I have researched potential locations, and I want to share that information with you.*

When speaking of qualifications, people often think of a long list of items from a resume. However, all you need to do to qualify yourself as a speaker, is to state in one sentence why you are speaking about the subject. Maybe you have ten years seniority at the company or perhaps you have an accounting background so they asked you to discuss the budget. Some people have qualifications just because they are the ones who researched the subject over the weekend.

The following will suffice as a qualifier:

I have been surfing the Internet and speaking to park managers for two days, and I have found several parks that would be perfect for our annual picnic.

Explain the Benefits of Listening

People want to know why they should listen to your presentation. Again, a long list of reasons to listen is not necessary. You just want to pique their interest so they are alert and willing to receive what you have to share. The following is an example:

The office picnic is a tradition of this company. Remember that the picnic is how the management team applauds our efforts through drawing names and giving gift baskets, extra vacation days, and bonus dollars. You are only eligible to get these things if you attend the event.

Preview the Main Points

Just state the two to five main points of your presentation in one or two sentences. Although it is fine to have one key main focus for your message, you don't want to confuse the audience by having too many sub-points. Also, you don't want more than five main points or this may cause information overload.

Today, we will discuss the three possible locations for the picnic. They are Noble Park, Fairmount Park, and Briley Park.

 PURPOSE OF THE CONCLUSION

If you end with a clear summary and a powerful creative closure, your audience members will feel good about you as a presenter and they will more likely remember your message.

Most conclusions should:

1st   Indicate the end of the presentation

2nd   Summarize the main points of your presentation

3rd   Have a creative closure

More dialogue-based presentations, like a "press conference" or an "interview," may not require all of the elements of the conclusion.

Ways to Indicate the End

Some will argue that saying "In conclusion" is a good way to let the audience know you are ending. However, those two words are so dull! You can use more creative vocabulary words that have the same effect:

- Always remember the three keys points I went over tonight.
- Never forget the three main reasons for drug abuse.
- There were two key points in this message.
- Let's review what we have learned.

Summarize the Main Points

The fourth element of your introduction (preview the main points), should be emphasized in the conclusion. You can re-state the main points word for word or you can paraphrase:

- Therefore, we have a choice of Noble Park, Fairmount Park, or Briley Park.
- Don't forget what I told you: Eat smaller portions, exercise at least three times a week, and stay away from too much sugar and white flour.
- If you remember nothing else, please remember that every child needs love, attention, and discipline.

Creative Closures

You never want to just end a presentation. You want people to remember your main points. You also want them to remember you as a great presenter. Therefore, you need to be memorable. You achieve this through a creative closure. This closure is the LAST thing out of your mouth. Do not keep talking and dragging out the conclusion. Once you get to the closure, you are finished!

Here are some types of creative closures (with or without humor).

RHETORICAL QUESTION OR SET OF QUESTIONS

Ask a question at the end that will make the audience remember your presentation.

- Now that you know the dangers, are you sure you want to try drugs?
- Do you want life . . . or death?
- So, if you had the chance to invest in the Roth IRA, why wouldn't you do it? Why would you still be afraid?

EMOTIONAL STATEMENT

Say something that they will remember. Make it a clear sentence or phrase and make sure you use effective pausing.

- Just stop it!

- When it comes to a college education, some people are willing to die for it.

- After all, if God brings you to it, He will bring you through it.

EMOTIONAL ACTION

Do something that they will remember.

- Don't spend your life doing this. (Point your finger out to the audience.) If you really want to change . . . do this. (Point your finger at your chest.)

- We are the best in the business so we need to be on top. (Stand on a chair.)

CALL TO ACT

Ask the audience members to do something or to refrain from doing something. Call them to act.

- Please wear your seatbelts.

- Stop smoking now!

- Please be aware of scam artists.

QUOTATION

You can close with a quotation that makes the audience think.

- My father always says, "People get exactly what they deserve."

- Former First Lady Hillary Clinton once said, "It takes a village."

- According to the June 10, 2008 edition of *My Money Magazine,* "people are not poor, just financially challenged." (fictitious quote)

REFER BACK TO THE INTRIGUE

A "refer back" is a wonderful closure where you mention the story, quote, statement, etc. that you used for the intrigue in the introduction.

- My mother is deceased, but she lived thirteen years with the cancer in remission. She was the strongest person I ever met, and I will never forget her love.

- The televangelist makes a good point; and for us, isn't choosing to be happy the best thing we can do for ourselves?

Remember, the introduction should make the audience want to listen. The conclusion should compel them to remember what you have said. If you begin with something intriguing and end with something creative and memorable, you and your message will be memorable too.

The Manuscript and Presentation Outlines

Outlines and connecting words and phrases allow you to structure your message so that your thoughts are clear and complete.

PURPOSE OF THE MANUSCRIPT OUTLINE

- Is in complete sentences
- Is a word-for-word outline of your speech
- Is structured well
- Is balanced: If you have an A, you should have a B, and so forth

MANUSCRIPT OUTLINE FORMAT

(For most informative and persuasive presentations)

This outline should include every single sentence or phrase from your presentation.

INTRODUCTION
  I. Intrigue the audience: question, short story, emotional statement or action, quotation.
  II. Introduce the topic and tell the audience why you are qualified to speak about it.
  III. Explain the benefit(s) of listening to the topic.
  IV. Preview the main points in one or two sentences.

Connecting words or phrases

BODY
  I. First main point
    A. Support
    B. More support

Connecting words or phrases

  II. Second main point
    A. Support
    B. More support

Connecting words or phrases

  III. Third main point
    A. Support
    B. More support

CONCLUSION

I. Indicate the end

II. Summarize your main points

III. Have a creative closure: question, emotional statement or action, call to act, quotation, refer back to the intrigue

CONNECTING WORDS AND PHRASES

I'll never forget a student's speech I heard years ago. I couldn't tell when the introduction ended and when the main points began. I kept waiting to hear a main point. She started the speech and then it was over. As a matter of fact, I still don't know what the main points were. I know I wasn't being overly critical because as I glanced around the classroom, most students looked perplexed. Some shrugged their shoulders, and some students even whispered, "Do you know what she's talking about?" As it turned out, the student was attempting to be creative by giving her speech as a story. The problem is that storytelling, although it is a form of speaking, is not appropriate as an entire traditional speech for a class or for a business setting where the purpose is to give information. A short story is wonderful as the intrigue for an introduction, as one of the main points in the body, or even as a way to indicate you are closing your presentation. However, a story should not be an entire speech unless entertainment is the only value.

A presentation needs structure. Outlining provides this structure. Within the outline, there are connecting words and phrases that indicate when you are going from one main point to the next main point. These connections help the message to have clarity. There is nothing worse than listening to someone speaking and then having to say, "Oh, he's talking about something else now. When did he finish with that last point?"

We sometimes refer to connecting words and phrases as transitions, signposts, or internal previews and summaries. Regardless of which ones you use, make sure your language clearly establishes that you are moving from one main point to the next main point.

Here are some examples of connecting words or phrases:

- *Now that we have discussed the pros and cons of Noble Park, let's examine the benefits of having the picnic at Fairmount Park.*

- *First, we could have the picnic at Noble Park.*

- *Fairmount Park is also an option.*

- *Finally, there is Briley Park.*

- *Stop what you are doing and listen to this last important point I need to make.*

- *If you remember nothing else today, remember this message.*

PURPOSE OF THE PRESENTATION OUTLINE

- Is a condensed version of the manuscript outline

- Contains only key words and phrases

- Visually looks like the manuscript outline, but bullets may be used instead of roman numerals, numbers, and letters

- Should not be more than two or three pages

- Is always typed

- Contains *mental reminders* for the speaker; i.e., when to insert the visual aid, to use eye contact, to relax, etc.

The biggest difference between the two outlines is length. You can write a ten-page manuscript outline at home. However, when you step onto the stage or in front of the room, you should have no more than two or three typed pages in a professional look-ing portfolio. You should never take a bunch of papers to the front of a room. You should never hold a stack of index cards for the audience to see. If you have practiced enough, you shouldn't need a lot of notes! A typed presentation outline in a portfolio is the best thing to have for a presentation. If you must use index cards, do not hold more than two white index cards as you present your message. You look unorganized and unprepared when you have a stack of notes with you. You should just have the presentation outline that contains any quotations you may use and the bullets of your main points.

PRESENTATION OUTLINE FORMAT

(For most informative and persuasive presentations)

This outline should only include key words or phrases and NOT complete sentences!

INTRODUCTION
- Intrigue audience: question, short story, emotional statement or action, quotation.
- Introduce the topic and tell the audience why you're qualified to speak about it.

- Explain the benefit(s) of listening to the topic.
- Preview the main points in one or two sentences.

Connecting words and phrases

BODY
- First main point
  - Support
  - More support

Connecting words or phrases

- Second main point
  - Support
  - More support

Connecting words or phrases

- Third main point
  - Support
  - More support

CONCLUSION
- Indicate the end
- Summarize your main points
- Have a creative closure: question, emotional statement or action, call to act, quotation, refer back to the intrigue

SAMPLE PRESENTATION OUTLINE

(Why a college student should consider a major in Communication)

***This outline should only include key words or phrases and NOT complete sentences!
It should also include "mental reminders."***

INTRODUCTION   (RELAX!!!!!!!!!!   YOU CAN DO THIS!!!!)
- How many of you are still unsure about . . . ?
- Communication is the study of . . . I have been in the field of communication . . .
- Today's companies want people with multiple skills and . . .
- I will first explain the communication model and its importance in the business . . . Potential careers . . . Why communication is a viable option . . .

Connecting words and phrases: First, what is this communication model that . . . ?

BODY

- ■ The sender . . . the receiver . . . the message . . . the channel . . .
  - • Many people don't realize . . . negotiation, resolving conflict, team communication . . . leadership skills . . . facilitator training all involve . . .
  - • It is a study that promotes healthy work environments . . . skills you learn are transferable to any . . . There are many organizations that request . . .

Connecting words or phrases: So what kind of job . . . ?

(***SHOW CHART WITH CAREERS LISTED***)

- ■ Graduates of this program enter numerous . . .
  - • Story about Maria . . . After graduate school, she entered the nonprofit . . .
  - • Story about James . . . This young man had a call on his life . . . He trained in . . . He went to Texas . . .
  - • Story about Karen . . . She found her passion in education after . . . The corporate world was . . . However, the knowledge of communication . . .

Connecting words or phrases: This area is a viable . . .

- ■ Are you someone who enjoys . . . ?
  - • A major in communication will allow you to be . . .
  - • If you know that you want to work for an organization that . . .

CONCLUSION   **(***RAISE THE PITCH—GET EMOTIONAL***)**

- ■ College has so much to offer . . .
- ■ If you are a student who is ready . . . remember what communication is . . . the possible careers . . . and why it could be a great . . .
- ■ Creative closure: . . . why be "pretty good" when you . . .

(PAUSE—CALM AND SINCERE) . . . can be the best?

(***CLOSE PORTFOLIO AND STEP AWAY—DON'T SAY THANK YOU***)

Do not say "thank you" as your creative closure! If you feel compelled to thank your audience, then thank the audience as you indicate the end of the presentation. The very last thing people should hear is your creative and memorable closure and not a bland "thank you."

If you sound professional, you will appear professional. If you sound unorganized, you will appear unorganized. You can pretend that you do things better at the last minute. You can pretend that you don't need to write a manuscript outline because you deliver better presentations by just "jotting down a few points" and then speaking "off the cuff." You can pretend that you only need the presentation outline with just your main points, because the rest is "in your head" and you don't want to sound so scripted.

Okay.

However, if anyone ever tells you that your presentation lacks organization, clarity, or appeal, remember that I wrote this chapter to prevent that from happening.

1. There's no substitution for preparation and for writing a complete presentation in a manuscript outline format. The manuscript outline helps you to write a message with a step-by-step process thus minimizing your potential to miss a key main point.

2. The connecting words and phrases are necessary to remind your listeners where you are in your message.

3. The presentation outline prevents you from reading your presentation at the time of delivery because it doesn't have complete sentences.

Each element serves a purpose. Each element is necessary to enhance clarity, vividness and retention value. Try to realize these three elements are not promoted in order to cause you stress; they are promoted in order to alleviate it.

Language Considerations When Preparing Your Outlines

Choose your words carefully. They should be clear, vivid and correct. The language you use should occasionally include the following to enhance message retention and audience excitement for your presentation:

- **Repetition:** Repeating a word or phrase over and over (Yes, we have problems in our country. From economics to crime, we have problems in our country. So many people have made positive contributions. So many people have given time, money and energy. We have made a lot of progress; but unfortunately, we still have major problems in our country.)

- **Antithesis:** Showing opposite ideas (Your actions are more important than your words; so it's not what you say about others, it's what others can honestly say about you.)

- **Alliteration:** Repeating the initial consonant sound (He prepared, practiced, and prayed.)

- **Parallelism:** Putting sentences or phrases in a similar pattern (Many college students are philanthropic. They are dedicated. They are compassionate. They are informed. They are the first to arrive and the last to leave. Sometimes students are not recognized for their contributions to humankind.)

- **Use of a Metaphor:** Vivid words that show the similarity between two different things (Her smile was sunshine.)

- **Use of a Simile:** Vivid words that show the similarity between two different things and the words "like" or "as" are used (Her smile was like sunshine.)

CHAPTER

4

Organizing and Affirming the Message

ORGANIZING THE MAIN POINTS

The only thing worse than a poor delivery is a poorly constructed manuscript. Too often people insist they know what they want to say but spend little time actually organizing their thoughts. This is why many audience members leave a presentation feeling unsatisfied or confused.

You can use several formal organizational patterns for the structure of a presentation. I offer the following most simplistic ways:

- List the points you wish to make and then put them into the order you wish to introduce them.
  - List your main points as *topics,* i.e., **I will share some tips for travel in the United States, tips for travel to Canada, and tips for travel overseas**.
  - Give the elements of the *problem* first and then *ways to solve* the problem, i.e., **Apathy** (first main point) **is a major problem regarding teenage drinking that often does not get discussed, but more exposure to the hazards** (second main point) **will help solve this problem**.
  - *State the causes* of some issue and then *cite the effects,* i.e., **Peer pressure** (first main point) **and family influences** (second main point) **cause young people to drink, and the result is a major increase of teen alcoholism** (third main point) **in this country**.
  - Discuss how something occurred *chronologically* over time and list each happening in a sequential order, with one behind the other, i.e., **West Eastern University had three major transformations which took place in 1972** (first main point), **in 1986** (second main point), **and in 2005** (third main point). **In 1972, the College of Engineering was built . . .**

- Do not have more than five main points for any presentation or you risk having your audience forget the key focus of your presentation due to information overload.

- I suggest two to four strong main points.

- After you list your main points in the proper order put support under each point. Make sure you can support whatever point you are trying to make. If you can't support it with examples, opinions, statistics, etc., then it's probably not a strong main point. Get rid of it and re-think your points.

LOCATING THE SUPPORT: LIBRARIES, ORGANIZATIONS, WEBSITES, INTERVIEWS

Regardless of your personal knowledge or experience, you need to validate your presentation through recent, unbiased, and documented evidence and sources of information. You can locate information at:

Libraries

Today, the Internet is the source people most utilize for finding evidence, but often the entire content of most books and journals are not on the Internet. You have to go to the library to get that information.

Organizations

You can get information from non-profit and for-profit organizations. You can write the organization or make requests via telephone or email. Most organizations are prepared to mail information to those who request it.

Shad Young conducts research on the Internet.

Websites

You can find a lot of support on the Internet. Websites are full of data and information that can aid your presentation; but make sure the website information is credible, unbiased, recent, and relevant!

Personal Interviews

Face-to-face or technology-induced interviews are wonderful for gathering support. Direct quotations taken from interviews with experts in a particular field, or quotations from people who have personal experiences that support your topic area, are excellent for a presentation.

CHOOSING THE RIGHT SUPPORT: STATISTICS, STUDIES, STORIES, TESTIMONIES, OPINIONS, EXAMPLES

Statistics

Statistical data as support of in-depth research on a subject is terrific for a presentation because you back up your opinion with solid and unbiased research.

Case Studies

You can also use information from case studies. You should cite case studies along with the authors and the dates of the studies, within the presentation.

Stories

A story from a documented source or a hypothetical story can serve as support to strengthen a speaker's message. Stories alone and without additional evidence are not as powerful as stories combined with other evidence. They are excellent to use especially if articulated with vivid language and a strong vocal delivery.

Testimonies

Personal testimonies are captivating because they invite the audience to know the person. Testimonies are compelling if the person testifying seems credible, honest, and sincere. Because the basis of the testimony is personal, people rarely dispute it. The speaker can give testimonies as part of his or her willingness to reveal personal information or retrieve them from the interviews of other people.

Opinions

A speaker's opinion is fine, but, again, it should not be the sole source of evidence. Audiences do not receive opinions well in an informative presentation. Persuasive presentations have personal opinions but they are best when combined with opinions from experts and opinions by lay people.

Examples

Examples help messages have clarity. Giving an example of something you are trying to explain will help to support your presentation. For example, this text—*Speaking With Ease*—has concepts that are easy for all adults to understand.

If you wish others to see you as a credible speaker/presenter, it is crucial for you to be aware of the location of the support and to be able to utilize the evidence you have found. Biased information in a presentation not only affects the credibility of the message but the credibility of the speaker. People won't listen to someone who has no evidence or to someone who presents slanted evidence. The use of a variety of sources, recent sources (within the past three years), and credible sources will increase the audience's perception of you as a presenter, thus increasing your chances of having your presentation respected and remembered.

REMEMBER: You must cite your sources with authors, dates, and the names of people or organizations within the presentation! You can't cite all of your sources after a presentation. It's also not a great idea to cite a full internet address.

Here are two fictitious examples of source citations:

- According to the Jump Magazine Website accessed July 12 of this year, over two thousand teenagers compete in the double-dutch national championship held in Chicago each year. *(fictitious source citation)*

- In a face-to-face interview with Dr. Bill Harkness on May 14, 2008, he stated that more women are starting to have congestive heart failure. *(fictitious interview)*

A presentation is not a research paper one reads. The audience must HEAR the bibliography. You can't attach a sheet of paper on the back of an oral presentation so cite your support during your presentation! Make sure your support is recent, accurate, clear, unbiased and complete!

Basic Delivery Concepts

Are you ready to practice the delivery? After you create the complete word for word manuscript outline, you must read it over and over until you know the material. When you know the material, create the presentation outline that includes the bullets of the main points, the mental reminders, and the direct quotations. Once these steps are completed, you are ready to practice the delivery of your presentation until you are positive that you will be perceived as comfortable, knowledgeable and memorable.

 # VERBAL CONSIDERATIONS

Volume

Speak up! It is annoying to strain to hear a speaker. You should not yell at your audience, but make sure everyone can hear you. If possible, practice at the location of the presentation. It is best to have someone listen in the back of the room to make sure everyone will be able to hear you.

Rate

Be aware of how fast or how slow you speak. If your speech is too fast, the audience may find it too difficult to listen to you. It may take too much energy to listen. If you speak too slowly, your delivery may drag and the presentation may become boring.

Pitch

It may not be fair but people perceive high-pitched voices as less credible. Try to keep the pitch low and vary the pitch to reflect the words you are using. Anger and excitement will raise the pitch and conveying sadness should cause your pitch to go down.

Pronunciation

Mispronounced words can cause a speaker to lose credibility. Don't be lazy with your language. You need to pronounce words clearly. It's "affidavit" not "affidavid."

Articulation and Enunciation

Articulation and enunciation have to do with how you form your speech sounds. Try not to slur your words together. Try to make sure the ends of words and the vowels of words are clear and correct. It's "tiger" not "tagger."

Appearance

How we look reflects how we feel. Usually a sloppy appearance means our lives are sloppy in several areas. When we look good we often feel good. Dress appropriately. Examine the occasion, the weather, the potential audience profile, the location, and so forth. Don't wear too many accessories and make sure your hair is neat and your shoes are polished and not run over!

Eye Contact

Image © AVAVA, 2009. Used under license from Shutterstock, Inc.

Please have prolonged eye contact with your audience. It's important to glance down while presenting and not glance up from reading. Having periods of prolonged eye contact with only occasional glances at your presentation outline, will make you appear more competent. Look at the three areas of a room: the right side, the left side, and the middle. Look at all three areas when you present your material. The people in the area you ignore, will become the least likely to remember your presentation. Make sure you hold your eye contact for several sentences before glancing at the next area in the room. Repeat this over and over without looking robotic. Relax your eyes and don't have a wide-eyed stare. Move your head and let your upper body relax while turning your head.

Planned Gestures

Use gestures that demonstrate descriptive words. Stretching your arms out to describe a "large house" will add clarity to your message. You should use planned gestures sparingly throughout the presentation.

Nervous Body Movements

Gestures have nothing to do with nervous body movements that are repetitive and distracting. RELAX! If there is a podium/lectern, place your hands gently on the top or on the sides unless you are using gestures. Standing behind a podium/lectern with your arms down by your waist looks awkward. If you don't want to put your hands on it, then step away and speak freestyle. Do NOT lean on the podium/lectern and try not to shift up and back or side to side. With or without a podium, try not to touch your face and hair. Try not to shake your leg. Do not play with coins or keys inside the pockets of your trousers/pants.

 # PRACTICING THE PRESENTATION

Here are some practice tips:

- Practice in front of a mirror.

- Practice in front of a small audience of HONEST friends.

- Record your presentation so you can see and hear it before you actually present.

- Practice in the room where you will give the presentation (if possible, arrive early).

- Practice looking at the three areas of the audience.

- Practice walking away from the podium while using controlled and planned hand gestures.

- Practice vocal gymnastics by reading poetry with pitch variations and emphasizing certain words to create excitement in your voice.

- Practice in clothing that is similar to what you will wear.

- Practice your delivery while using all of your presentation aids and make sure your aids don't keep you from having a fluid delivery.

The message is important, but if your delivery is dull and you appear unprepared and unenthusiastic, the audience may only remember one key point: *Thank goodness this person has stopped speaking.* Don't leave your audience with that impression. Leave your audience wanting to know more about you and more about your message.

Presentation
Aids

PURPOSE

You can utilize presentation aids to help the audience comprehend specific concepts or steps from your speech; however, their execution can 'make' or 'break' a presentation. While professional and creatively designed presentation aids can enhance the audience's experience with the speaker, poorly constructed aids that are used incorrectly can actually detract from your message, leading to audience confusion and detachment. Consider using a presentation aid when:

- Presenting technical data or other quantitative data (via a chart or graph)
- Referring to a particular location or place (via a map)
- 'Words' are simply not enough (via a powerful image)
- Describing a particular process or skill (via your own demonstration)
- Outlining specific points of the speech (via a handout, poster, etc.)
- Demonstrating your *ethos* (via a great execution of your presentation aids)

TYPES AND PROPER USE

Charts, Posters, and Graphs

Charts, posters and graphs are inexpensive and highly effective if created properly and used correctly. You can set them up and dismantle them with little effort, and they are ideal for small audiences, a sales pitch, and locations where power sources and/or technology are inconvenient. Be sure there is a balance of color and text and that all words, numbers, and images are large enough for the audience members in the last row to easily see without squinting.

PowerPoint and Multimedia

For larger audiences, consider using technology to help convey your supporting data, details, and images. PowerPoint, overhead transparencies, or slideshows can help promote professionalism and creativity. However, one must use caution in balancing the speaker's presence with the slides' visual impression. All visual aids should simply 'accompany' the speaker's words with important details and purposeful images. While PowerPoint has become the standard medium for presentation aids in the twenty-first century, it has also generated considerable criticism because speakers overuse and abuse the format, thus creating distractions that have too much animation and too much text. Remember, your goal is to create and execute a dynamic and audience-centered presentation. Turning your back and reading text from a screen will result in alienating your audience and ruining your chances for success.

Consider the following when creating PowerPoint slides:

- Remember the 5 × 5 rule—no more than five words per line and five lines per slide (that would be 25 words maximum per slide).

- Try to limit yourself to one slide per minute of delivery.

- Be sure your colors and fonts reflect the tone of the presentation (professional versus comical) and help the audience read the information without making them strain their eyes.

- Limit the sound and animation to the absolute minimum. Let your words and delivery style—not the technology—impress your audience.

- Rehearse the timing and practice the execution.

Objects and Models

Objects, if large enough for all to see, are wonderful visual aids! Audience members get involved in the message when they get to see something tossed around or used to demonstrate some new technique, concept, or item. If the object is too large or too valuable, consider a model that will allow you to communicate the same information as if the original object was there. Be sure the model is well-constructed and clearly represents the item you wish to explain. Also, be sure objects and models are large enough to see; and make sure they do not distract the audience.

Graduate student April R. Payne correctly uses her presentation aid. She points to the object while maintaining eye contact with the audience. She does NOT talk to the object!

Photographs and Handouts

Avoid passing around photographs and handouts before or during a presentation! If you can't enlarge photos or display them via PowerPoint so that everyone in the audience can see them; hold them up briefly during the presentation and invite the audience to view them after you finish. This way they are still aiding the presentation; people will actually see them, but they will not cause a distraction while you are speaking.

Handouts can be beneficial since audience members can record notes on them and refer back to your speech content at a later time. However, if audience members see what your entire speech is about, they can also 'tune you out.' Avoid divulging the entire speech via your outline or PowerPoint printouts and handouts. If you need to supply a small audience with technical and/or detailed information on one or two handouts, distribute each handout as you reach the specific moment in the presentation. With larger audiences or with three or more handouts, supply a folder with all handouts clearly titled and paginated for easy retrieval and reference during the presentation. Ask your audience to keep the folder closed until you tell them to open it. I usually play a game and award prizes to people who catch people reading ahead. Prizes energize presentations, and they motivate audience members to pay attention. I make sure they do not focus on catching people by also awarding prizes to those who retain the most information.

Whatever you do, when it comes to written material, proofread anything you put on display. Misspelled words in big letters on a PowerPoint screen or on a typed handout could hurt your credibility.

Video and Audio (Audio encompasses CDs as well)

Depending upon the length of time you have to present your material, multimedia can serve as a nice diversion from all of the speaking you have to do. A funny clip can liven up a presentation. A dramatic clip or a sound bite can help people to focus on your message. Make sure that you explain what people will see or hear, and make sure you clearly explain the purpose for presenting the clip before and after you play it. You must set it up and summarize its significance. In most speaking situations, your total length of time for these aids should take no more than 10% of your total presentation time.

Your Own Body and Live Models

During demonstration ("how to") speeches, you may find the need to demonstrate a particular task in order for your audience to visualize and comprehend your message.

This can be very engaging for an audience and can allow you an opportunity to move around and offer some dynamic energy. Regardless of the task, you should keep your attention focused on your audience either through eye contact or words. Never allow a gap of 'dead time' while you complete a task. Talk the audience through it. If you need to fill some time while you accomplish the task, offer some insight about the history of your topic, an interesting factoid, or an anecdote.

If the presentation requires a significant amount of activity or movement, you may want to consider using live models to demonstrate while you focus on the audience. Always prepare and rehearse beforehand with any person you want to incorporate into the presentation and be sure he or she understands your goals and objectives. Be very clear with your live models as to when you will use them during the presentation, how and where they will enact the activity, and how they should enter and leave the performance area.

Speak to your models about how they should dress and have them arrive early so you can instruct them and clarify any issues before presenting. Try not to use an uninformed or unprepared 'volunteer' from the audience. You are not doing a hypnotist act.

Regardless of the type of presentation aid, remember the following:

Aids should:

- Create vivid images and concrete meanings

- Assist the audience with message retention

- Reflect professionalism and enthusiasm for one's presentation

- Help demonstrate proficiency for presentational speaking

- Be dynamic and clearly reflect their purpose

- Never be displayed throughout the entire presentation

- Be large enough for everyone in the audience to see them

- Be used during every dress rehearsal

- Should have some color

Chapter written by Coel Coleman and Yastremski

CHAPTER

7

Inspirational, Informative, and Persuasive Presentations

THE ACCEPTANCE OF AN AWARD OR GIFT

(*Also see* The Presentation of an Award or Gift)

Most awards or gifts indicate that someone is recognized while others are not. Therefore, the audience consists of those who are happy for the recipient, and those who are possibly resentful or jealous. If you receive an award or gift in front of an audience, you will be expected to express your gratitude. Be as brief and gracious as possible. Acknowledge those who helped you to achieve your success. Always thank the person who presented the award/gift and those who were instrumental in choosing you over the other candidates. Although taken for granted, this speech should not be neglected! A poorly prepared speech of acceptance is insulting to those who took the time to consider you as an asset. A poor acceptance screams: "Gee thanks but thanking you takes too much thought and effort to overcome my fear of speaking so I'm just saying 'thanks a lot' . . . I hope that's good enough." You need to make the presenter glad he or she chose you to be the recipient.

Corporate Development Specialist and Professor of Communication Karen Hill Johnson, created a manuscript outline for this very important presentation. Professor Johnson has years of experience in education, sales, and event planning where awards are often presented and accepted. (See her sample outline for The Presentation of an Award or Gift later in this chapter.)

Suggested Aids

None are needed, but if you have time to prepare a great speech of acceptance you can be creative and use:

- An enlarged photograph of yourself, "before and after," showing how much you have changed physically or emotionally
- An item of clothing to highlight your enthusiasm for the award/gift (a hat that has "I LOVE YOU" on it)

A SAMPLE MANUSCRIPT OUTLINE
for
The Acceptance of an Award or Gift

INTRODUCTION

I. "The dream begins with a teacher who believes in you, who tugs and pushes and leads you to the next plateau, sometimes poking you with a sharp stick called 'truth.'" Dan Rather. **(Intrigue: emotional statement)**

II. Mr. Rather was correct when it comes to the leadership role of teachers.
(Introduce the topic)

III. Teaching is my passion and to be recognized for it, is quite an honor.
(Tell why you are qualified to speak)

IV. Today, I would like to thank those who made the dream of teaching a reality before finally sharing with you why I am so very passionate about what I do.
(Preview the main points)

Connecting words or phrases: First, a round of thanks.

BODY

I. I must thank my Lord and Savior as I know him, Jesus Christ, my parents, my dear husband and finally, the students of the Speech Communication Department of West Eastern University.

    A. Many times doubt and discouragement may have been an obstacle but my faith has pulled me through. Many times it was Jesus pulling me through those late nights of running out of red ink pens and grading those journals.

    B. To my parents, thank you for allowing me to be creative and for pushing me to always give 110% in all I do.

    C. Thanks to my dear husband for your unconditional love and unending support of my career ... I love you.

    D. To my dear students, this award would not be possible if it were not for you. Thank you for listening to my words of wisdom and my honest critiques. All of you are very special to me and all of you have touched my life in a very special way.

    (First main point with support)

Connecting words or phrases: I am able to touch the lives of my students because I answered my calling.

II. Teaching is not a job; it's a calling.

    A. I am truly blessed to be a professor, especially in the field of Communication at West Eastern University.

        1. This school and the department in which I serve are phenomenal!

    B. I am encouraged to be myself and I utilize my strengths to serve the students and the university.

        1. When others are compelled to clone their teaching style to fit an administrative or selfish personal agenda, it is a joy to work for people who embrace diversity within the curriculum and within minds of those who attempt to improve it.

    C. I urge all of you to consider your passion and answer your own personal calling.

    (Second main point with support)

CONCLUSION

I. It is an honor to touch the lives of so many; and it is an exceptional honor to be awarded the Profound Professor Award of 2008.

(Indicate the end)

II. I'll never forget those who helped me to stretch my imagination for a career that I love so much.

(Summarize your main points)

III. The dream may begin with the teacher who motivates you, but the reality begins when the student answers the challenge, from the teacher who presents . . . the truth.

(Creative closure: emotional statement)

Manuscript outline submitted by:
Karen Hill Johnson, M.S.
Corporate Development Specialist
Professor of Communication
Mid-Continent University

THE ANNOUNCEMENT

So many announcements are made every year! However, many announcements have incorrect and incomplete information that cause frustration, a lack of attendance at functions and missed opportunities. Announcements should be brief, concise, and complete.

Announcements are still presentations but in their simplest form. Sporting events, holiday celebrations, employment situations, etc. are all occasions that call for announcements. Make sure that you are knowledgeable about the announcement.

Rehearsing an announcement is not far-fetched. Stumbles, poor volume and rate, backtracking, etc. can cause the message to be misconstrued or lost. People miss meetings or they show up late because of poor announcements! Locations and times are so important. These must be stated clearly or confusion is likely to occur.

Image © Dmitriy Shironosov, 2009. Used under license from Shutterstock, Inc.

Announcements should be made where everyone in the room can see you and hear you.

Suggested Aids

None are needed, but if you want to generate a lot of interest in an event you could:

- Show a picture of the location

- Put on an item of clothing to emphasize the message

- Use multi-media to show a location or a picture that will create strong emotions

---

A SAMPLE MANUSCRIPT OUTLINE

for

The Announcement

(BASIC ORGANIZATION INFORMATION)

INTRODUCTION

I. You can eat, drink and be happy!

(Intrigue: emotional statement)

BODY

I. The Social Committee is holding a Chat-N-Chew Reception for all members on Friday, September 19th at 6:00 P.M. at the Doubletree Hotel.

(Who, What, When, Where)

II. Everyone is invited to attend this casual event at the end of our work day. Please sign the sheet at the front desk so we know how much food to order. There will be vegetarian options too. There is no charge for this reception but you will not be permitted to attend if you don't sign up by September 15th.

(Details and Cost)

III. If you wish to unwind after a long week and enjoy good food with good people, join us for this company event.

(Benefit for the listener)

CONCLUSION

Remember September 19th at 6:00 P.M. at the Doubletree. Let's Chat. Let's Chew. Let's have a good time!

(Summary and closures: emotional statements)

Coel Coleman

A SAMPLE MANUSCRIPT OUTLINE

for

The Announcement

(MEMBER/EMPLOYEE RECOGNITION)

INTRODUCTION

  I. He's the first to come to work and the last to leave.
    (Intrigue: emotional statement)

  II. Ever since he stepped into this building just a year ago, he has been a productive team player and certainly one who deserves recognition for this last quarter. I'm glad I hired him!
    (Introduce the topic and tell why you're qualified to speak)

  III. Mike Edwards is an outstanding employee and an even greater person.
    (Preview the main points)

BODY

  I. When Mike applied, he told me that he wanted to be excited about coming to work each day.

    A. He had jobs that he enjoyed but he wanted a career and a place of employment that excited and challenged him.

      1. When I told him that we tried to be client and employee-centered, you could see the relief in his eyes.

      2. Almost immediately, he started assuring me that he wasn't afraid of hard work and long hours. Of course that excited me!

    B. He started work the next day and consistently produced quality written material. He knows numbers and he's the best in the business!

      1. After a few months, I noticed that he was getting respect from you, his co-workers and his superiors.

      2. This led me to realize that he was not just a team player but a leader.

      3. As a manager, he has done a wonderful job motivating his team and getting the numbers needed to satisfy the goal.

    (First main point with support)

Connecting words or phrases: But Mike's ability to excel in the workplace is surpassed by his contributions to humankind.

  II. He is a community visionary.

    A. He volunteers at the local YMCA where he teaches martial arts and tennis to young children.

       I. He is a member of the PTA, an executive board member for several organizations and he volunteers at his church.

    B. He was a beneficiary of the United Way when he was boy scout so he was passionate about being the chairperson of this year's fundraising drive.

        I. His efforts generated the largest amount raised over the past twenty years in this city ... close to $250,000!

        (Second main point with support)

CONCLUSION

  I. As we close out another term, we have to recognize those who have helped us reach new levels of success.
    (Indicate the end)

  II. Mike Edwards is one of those people ... one who not only gives to this company but who also gives to this community.
    (Summarize your main points)

  III. As he goes home tonight to that beautiful wife and his two adorable children, I want him to know that we appreciate him almost as much as they do! Everyone, let's thank Mike for all that he does ... and for all that he is!
    (Creative closures: emotional statements)

Coel Coleman

THE DEBATE

There are so many forms of debate: Lincoln Douglas, Cross Examination, Academic, Individual and Team Parliamentary, NEDA, NDT, etc. Therefore, the audiences will vary according to the type of debate and according to the debate function. If the debate is

for a school competition, then the audience will be made up of academic personnel and the debater's peers. If the debate is for a public political forum, then the audience will be made up of political figures, media people and the general public. Know why you are debating and know what form of debate will be utilized. Adjust your style and language to fit the audience and purpose for the argumentation. Sometimes you are compelled to

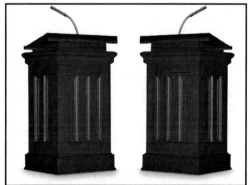

debate in a room that is not conducive for argumentation. If so, you must adjust the volume and tone of your voice or you could be annoying to the human ear. You don't want to sound like you are screaming at your audience and you also don't want to bore your audience because you're too soft. Debates are emotional so the energy must be there; but don't be too overwhelming or you will turn off the audience and the persuasion won't be effective.

Practice your individual speeches, which are often called "constructives" or "affirmative arguments." The question and answer (cross examination) period cannot be formally rehearsed, but you can have someone ask plausible questions to test your your ability to answer quickly and succinctly. You want to practice answering questions without becoming flustered or confused. You don't want to look unprepared.

In the following manuscript, educator and consultant David A. Yastremski, M.S. offers this example of an academic debate for a classroom setting. Professor Yastremski still directs an award-winning speech and debate program in New Jersey. He has also served as an adjunct professor of speech communication at Seton Hall University.

Suggested Aids

Having written or typed "evidence" to actually give to the opposing side during a debate is usually the main presentation aid. Some other possible aids include:

- Handouts, documents, or index cards with quotations from experts or citations from recent and credible sources

- Any object, like an apple that's cut up for a debate on education to show how educators are divided on the importance of standardized tests

---

A SAMPLE MANUSCRIPT OUTLINE
for
The Debate

(A standard academic debate for a class)

The organization names, website citations, quotations, names of characters, and statistics in this outline are fictitious. Any similarities to people or information are a coincidence.

SPEAKER FOR THE AFFIRMATIVE SIDE

INTRODUCTION

I. Colleen had a 4.0 grade point average, but Colleen scored low on the national standardized test. Colleen was president of her senior class, but Colleen scored low on the

national standardized test. Colleen went to college but Colleen did not get into the college she wanted to go to ... because Colleen scored low on the national standardized test. Colleen was an excellent student, class leader, community volunteer, member of several athletic teams and philanthropic organizations, but when it came down to college admissions, some universities only noticed that Colleen scored low on her standardized test. That is why I stand "Resolved, that standardized tests, should not be considered a part of a student's college admissions' application."
(Intrigue: short story plus the resolution)

II. This debate can be won by looking at the greater good for the greater amount of people. More people will benefit from removing standardized tests as proof of one's aptitude for college. I'll explain how the tests do not demonstrate one's tenacity or ability to excel; and then I'll propose how the test questions are structured to favor certain groups of people thus leaving others at a gross disadvantage.
(State the criteria and preview the main points)

BODY

I. There are several reasons why the use of standardized tests should be abolished in the college admissions' process.

A. First, the tests do not demonstrate a person's creativity, passion, and work ethic. All three are extremely important to succeed in the college classroom. For example, the National Coalition for Public Schools' website last updated on July 31, 2008, states that "standardized tests, do not adequately measure those skills that colleges are seeking such as creativity, leadership, and work ethic. They don't even measure a student's intelligence—just the ability to take a test." Clearly, college classrooms are not simply about tests. Classrooms are about discussions, seminars, dialogue, and a complete academic and intellectual experience. How can a test measure that?

B. In addition, the United States Commission on Testing and Assessment reports that standardized testing presents many flaws. The Commission states "all the major standardized tests fail to sufficiently predict a student's potential success in college, thus making a student's high school experience, including coursework and grades, the best predictor of student success." This was taken from the Commission's website accessed on July 20th. Clearly, standardized tests are not valid predictors of success and should not be factored into the college admissions' process.
(First main point with support)

Connecting words or phrases: Then, there is bias.

II. Standardized tests are biased against certain minority populations.

A. On average, African-American and Hispanic-American students score less than their white counterparts on all the standardized tests by up to 300 points. In addition, boys typically outperform girls on the tests according to the United States Commission on Testing and Assessment.

Inspirational, Informative, and Persuasive Presentations **47**

Murray State graduate student Luke Finck (left) and undergraduate student Tyler Smith, prepare for their team parliamentary debate.

B. Actually, the tests are designed to favor Caucasian students over minority students. As cited in the 2008 National Study of Standardized Tests, conducted by Ridge University, Glenn Stephens, executive director of the Standard Examination Foundation, conducted an analysis in 2007 where he examined answers from three national test administrations. Stephens' findings suggest that questions on all the major tests favor upper and upper-middle class, Caucasian students. In all three major standardized testing situations, test questions and reading selections were tailored for higher socio-economic experiences, thus creating a significant bias.

C. Stephens' study also emphasized the availability for test prep courses and in-school test prep programs. These are more available for students in high socio-economic groups.

(Second main point with support)

CONCLUSION

I. Because standardized tests do not serve as a valid predictor of college success, and because they are biased against minority and lower socio-economic groups, I stand resolved: That standardized tests should not be considered a part of a student's college application.

(Indicate the end and summarize main points)

II. After all, how many visionaries have we lost because we insist on ignoring diverse talents in favor of promoting rigid and slanted standards where only the privileged few can succeed?

(Creative closure: rhetorical question)

SPEAKER FOR THE NEGATIVE SIDE

INTRODUCTION

I. While we can sympathize with the "Colleens" of the world, my opponent would like you to believe that college admissions' officers make their decisions on standardized tests alone; however, this narrow-minded premise is unfounded. For this reason, I stand to negate the resolution and I support the use of standardized tests as a part of the college admissions' process.

(Intrigue: emotional statement plus the resolution)

II. I would like to start by stating that it is not the negative's burden to prove that standardized tests should be the only factor for college admissions. Tests should be "considered," as the resolution states, in a student's application for college. The negative position is that along with grades, course selection, and other factors including extra-curricular involvement and community service, standardized tests provide a more clear and reliable picture of applicants.

(Preview the main points)

BODY

I. According to the Domestic and International News Source website, dated March 6th, several research studies suggest that a student's transcript, extra-curricular experiences, and standardized test scores, when used together—are the best indicators of college success.

A. This is primarily due to course titles and grade inflation in some American High Schools that skew the selection criteria. According to Tatiana Glam of the College Resource Center at Mendham University, "due to pressures from parents and the competitive college application process, many schools have seen an increase in grade inflation cases." Clearly grade inflation has proven to be a prime concern and an obstacle for college personnel who make decisions about student applications.

B. Catherine Nore, an independent college counselor, agrees, as cited in the 2008 Metro News Report. "Colleges and universities are finding an increasing amount of cases where grade inflation affects a student's overall transcript and grade point average. A student earning a 4.0 average at one high school, may have only achieved a 3.0 at another. Everything from course selections, teacher selections, and assessment strategies, impact a transcript and grade point average."

(First main point with support)

Connecting words or phrases: Clearly, standardized tests offer one measure that transcends issues of grade inflation.

II. While it should not be the only standard of measurement for one's acceptance or denial, clearly, it offers the most objective picture of a student's aptitude, especially considering the large amount of applications that many universities receive.

A. According to JK Matthews, in his book entitled *The Fair Decisions,* while smaller liberal arts schools may have the resources and staff to explore each candidate more thoroughly, larger schools do not have the staff or the resources to conduct such in-depth evaluations of thousands of applicants. Larger schools need an objective measure to help narrow the pool of applicants." According to Ken Roberts, director of the

Standardized Test Association, "standardized tests provide the most fair national standard available for these schools.

B. In addition, several new standardized tests are instituting open-ended assessment strategies. These new sections have recently been touted by the New Jersey State University, providing the first independent analysis of the new standardized test formats. As stated by the university's website, accessed on June 20th of this year, Rob Askew, professor of education, states that the findings suggest that universities should not ignore the new standardized test formats. Colleges that refuse to use the new standardized test formats are relinquishing an opportunity to build a quality class of students who will perform better. With higher graduation rates and more insightful class experiences, the media's attack on standardized tests could eventually lead to substandard classes and the reduced quality of education.

(Second main point with support)

CONCLUSION

I. Because standardized tests have proven to be a positive influence in the college admissions process and new formats are being discovered each year, I stand in negation of "Resolved, that standardized tests, should not be considered a part of a student's college admissions application."

(Indicate the end and summarize your main points)

II. Historically, tests have been necessary to objectively assess knowledge. Why in the world would we want to ignore or try to invalidate their importance?

(Creative closure: question)

CROSS–EXAMINATION

AFFIRMATIVE: Do you not agree that racial bias exists when analyzing standardized test scores?

NEGATIVE: There may be some differentiation in performance; however, that does not mean that colleges should overrule the benefits of testing as an objective standard in the college admissions process.

AFFIRMATIVE: How can you assert that something, which promotes racial bias, serves as an objective standard?

NEGATIVE: What I mean is that while an applicant can provide all of his or her grades, courses, extracurricular activities, and community service projects, along with essays, the only objective comparative measurements with students and teachers from other schools in other states, are the standardized tests.

AFFIRMATIVE: Speaking of socio-economic concerns, isn't it true that students who come from higher socio-economic areas typically perform better on the exams.

NEGATIVE: That may be true; however, there are many variables, which influence such statistics other than the test performance.

AFFIRMATIVE: Like the amount of money that students and parents can afford to spend on preparation courses?

NEGATIVE: Money is a factor along with the parents' educational background, support at home, quality of instruction in schools, student test anxiety, etc. Many variables affect a student's performance on exams. No one is claiming that the playing field is equal in all cases; however, as I stated in my case, these tests should remain as one variable to consider for schools that may need a comparative form of measurement to help highlight strengths and weaknesses of student applications.

AFFIRMATIVE: Your quote about the standardized tests being the most fair national standard comes from Ken Roberts, director of the Standardized Test Association, correct?

NEGATIVE: Yes

AFFIRMATIVE: Isn't the Standardized Test Association the company that writes and promotes several different standardized tests?

NEGATIVE: Yes

AFFIRMATIVE: Shouldn't that create suspicion that he may be biased?

NEGATIVE: Sure, it can raise suspicion; however, the study involved a large sample and valid research techniques; and as I stated in my case, the benefits of standardized tests have been corroborated by the New Jersey State University in an independent analysis.

AFFIRMATIVE: Thank you.

NEGATIVE REBUTTAL

I. Thank you for listening to this debate. I give thanks to my opponent for giving some good arguments. The problem is that my opponent spent the whole debate confused about what the resolution implies. As the negative, I don't have to advocate that standardized tests should be the only form of measurement in the college application process. **(Indicate the end)**

II. There was this insistence that standardized tests are biased. Well, the entire admissions process can be labeled as 'biased' but do we do away with the process? There must be an objective standard of measurement. In addition, let me point to the Domestic and International News Source website accessed July 12th 2008, where it is clearly stated that standardized tests, in combination with transcripts and extra-curricular experiences, provide the best prediction of college success. **(Final refutation of opponent's points)**

III. I must restate that standardized tests should not be the sole factor in determining success. It is just one factor. An excellent student will get to go to college. However, universities, especially those with great reputations, have a right to use something that predicts whether a person can keep up with a rigorous course load. Standardized tests do show some indication as to whether a person has a strong aptitude for testing within an academic environment. Colleen is a student who deserves a chance to have an education. However, she most likely doesn't deserve an acceptance for every college. She deserves an acceptance to those schools where her qualifications meet the criteria. Unfortunately, not every hardworking student can get into every university; he or she has to earn it.
(Summary and creative closures: emotional statements)

AFFIRMATIVE REBUTTAL

(The affirmative side always goes last in a debate)

I. Again, let me thank you for listening to this debate. I thank my worthy opponent for some excellent clash. However, her points are still flawed.
(Indicate the end)

II. My opponent cites biased sources to promote biased practices. The rationale that consideration is not the same as a sole benchmark does not negate the fact that it's still a major factor for students who through no fault of their own, are disadvantaged.
(Final refutation of opponent's points)

III. The greater good of educating all of America for the greater amount of people cannot be served as long as biased standardized tests are utilized. It's time to allow intelligent and motivated students like Colleen to pursue a quality education. It's time to open our minds and to stop closing doors to these hardworking young people. It's time to makes changes to an old system that still prevents many outstanding students from going to the best colleges . . . just because of one . . . lousy . . . test.
(Summary and creative closure: emotional statements)

Manuscript outline submitted by:
David A. Yastremski, M.S.
Educator and Consultant
Bernards Township Public Schools
Basking Ridge, New Jersey

 # THE DEDICATION

Most dedications are public dedications with diverse audiences. Local, regional or national dignitaries are usually present. A dedication can be private with family and friends but usually when something is dedicated to someone, there is often a public display of gratitude. This type of presentation is just one element of the celebration.

You often see ribbon-cuttings or the breaking of a champagne bottle at dedications. Unlike the tribute, the dedication involves something being named after a person or something being honored for years to come. The tribute is a commemorative presentation without a building, holiday, or event being named for that person or concept.

Image © Mike Flippo, 2009. Used under license from Shutterstock, Inc.

Most likely, technology will not be available unless it is a very prominent dedication with a very large audience. Most local dedications involve less than 200 people so technical capabilities are unnecessary. However, it is more likely than not that the media will be there so be able to present your material without being influenced by cameras or journalists running around in front of you. Regardless of your surroundings, speak up!

This IS a presentation. You must practice. If you know you will be outside, make sure you practice outside in the attire you will be wearing. You don't want any surprises like clothes blowing around or unplanned noises. Be able to raise or lower your voice when distractions occur outside. Be prepared by practicing in the actual speaking environment ahead of time.

Suggested Aids

- A dollar bill to represent the money spent to create the new structure

- An article of clothing with the name of the honoree on the front or a picture of the new structure/equipment, etc. on the front

---

A SAMPLE MANUSCRIPT OUTLINE
for
The Dedication

INTRODUCTION

I. It was once a dream deferred; today it's a dream realized.
(Intrigue: emotional statement)

II. Mayor Jones, distinguished guests, community members and friends. Ten years ago, this building was just a vision in the mind of Mr. Coel. I was there when he made the proposal at the city council meeting.
(Introduce the topic and tell why you are qualified to speak)

III. Today, we celebrate that vision as we officially open this new community center that will benefit all of us.

(Explain the benefits of listening)

IV. The Raphael M. Coel Community Center represents love, trust and hope.

(Preview the main points)

Connecting words and phrases: As we look at this building, we know that our local leaders love this community and those who reside within its borders.

BODY

I. The leaders fought long and hard to get this center built.

   A. It took many meetings and many hours to get financial and governmental support.

   B. The leaders showed their love by working hard and fighting for this building.

   (First main point with support)

Connecting words and phrases: As we look at this building, we know our local leaders can be trusted to honor our needs and requests.

II. Many of us were skeptical at first. However, after just a short period of time, our leaders were answering our phone calls, our letters and our emails.

   A. Soon, we realized that they were not just trying to make us think they cared ... They actually cared!

   B. Our leaders showed us that they do care and they can be trusted!

   (Second main point with support)

Connecting words and phrases: As we look at this building, we have hope in the leaders we have now and those who are destined to follow.

III. When you lose hope, you lose everything.

   A. It's wonderful to know we have hope. As we gather to continue improving this community, it's amazing to realize that we are different.

   B. We are a city of hope and not of discouragement.

   C. Our leaders are strong and vigilant thus teaching our children the value of hard work and honest communications.

   (Third main point with support)

CONCLUSION

I. So, now we can go forth and continue to build upon Mr. Coel's vision.

(Indicate the end)

II. We have three things we can hold in our hearts and our minds. We have a community in which our children can find love ... trust ... and hope!

(Summary and creative closures: emotional statement)

Coel Coleman

THE DEMONSTRATION

Demonstrations are so neglected. Too often, presenters are convinced that all they have to do is a "show and tell" performance. Well, that's appropriate for first grade but an adult audience expects and deserves more.

Make sure you have great eye contact as you demonstrate.

These presentations are often confusing, unorganized and boring because without writing a structured systematic manuscript (chronological order) and then thinking that practice is silly, the speaker will probably stumble over words, get the steps out of order or have trouble with any objects that are used for the demonstration. Practicing a demonstration speech requires patience. You have to go over the steps of the demonstration until the actions and delivery are fluid and compelling.

Suggested Aids

Show whatever you are attempting to demonstrate. Don't just talk about something. You need to use the objects and physically demonstrate the actions you wish your audience to learn. You can't talk about jujitsu; you have to show the audience certain manipulations. You can't tell us how to throw a basketball without bringing a ball with you and showing us how to hold the ball and how to actually throw it.

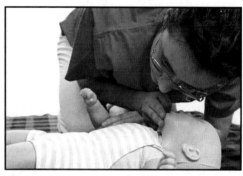

Objects/models that are used for demonstration need to be large enough for everyone to see them.

A SAMPLE MANUSCRIPT OUTLINE
for
The Demonstration

INTRODUCTION

I. Are you sure you deliver messages effectively and don't hypnotize your audiences with constant pacing and nervous movements?
   (Intrigue: rhetorical question)

II. Public speaking causes so much fear. I have taught and studied the art of public speaking for over twenty years and I want to show you some ways to more effectively control your body when you deliver a speech.

(Introduce the topic and tell why you are qualified to speak)

III. Even if you don't personally have speech anxiety, a few tips about how to improve one's ability to communicate should be beneficial to all of those who wish to excel in or out of the workplace.

(Explain the benefits of listening)

IV. I will demonstrate how your body should move while speaking at a podium and how your posture should be if you speak freestyle.

(Preview the main points)

Connecting words and phrases: This is just a podium.

BODY
   I. It looks harmless to me; but for some, it's worse than standing behind a wolf.

   A. There is something about standing behind a podium that makes some people feel claustrophobic and trapped. Others feel weak, naked and on display for the entire world to see.

   1. Regardless, of how you feel, the first thing you do is approach the podium with confidence even if you feel horrible. Fake it! Don't sigh and drag your feet like this. (demonstrate)

   2. Instead, when you stand up, walk straight with poise and control. (demonstrate) Make sure you hold your portfolio at your side.

   3. Secondly, when you get to the podium, open your portfolio and arrange your presentation outline so you won't have to fumble with it. It's best to have just two typed pages so you never have to move the paper. However, if you have more than two pages, stack the pages on your left side and gently slide the left page to the right side as you finish each page, like this. (demonstrate) You should NEVER staple an outline and have to turn pages. That doesn't look as professional as an indiscreet sliding of a page from left to right. (demonstrate again)

   4. Finally, if you can have a lavaliere microphone, make sure you walk away from the podium at least twice … like this. (demonstrate) You want to walk once or twice to the left of the podium and once or twice to the right side of the podium. This way, people are not forced to stare at one spot and it allows for you to seem more personable and less rigid.

Connecting words and phrases: Freestyle is often perceived as easier until one has to actually assess his or her performance.

II. Some students are so thrilled when I tell them they get to "walk" during a speech until I tell them that walking doesn't mean pacing.

    A. When you are away from any type of podium or lectern, you are totally exposed to your audience. Once nerves come into play, you may want to start walking back and forth across the room or the stage. This will hypnotize your audience and some will zone out to what you are saying because they have been put into a trance!

    B. Watch me. (demonstrate) Speak away from the podium and have your upper body move while your lower body is still. As your eye contact goes from the left side, to the middle, to the right side of the room, only your upper body and your head need to move. (demonstrate)

    C. Secondly, use your hands to effectively gesture like this (demonstrate). However, do not use your hands in insecure ways like this. (demonstrate) Clasping four fingers with your other hand, rubbing the sides of your thighs, playing with keys or coins that are in your pockets, and the repetitive pounding of your fist into the palm of the other hand, are all insecure movements.

CONCLUSION

  I. So, you can keep doing what you are doing or you can challenge yourselves to be better presenters.

    (Indicate the end)

  II. Practice speaking with and without a podium/lectern and pay attention to your body language and planned gestures.

    (Summarize your main points)

  III. Don't guess or assume; practice so that you can be positive that you are delivering your messages effectively so that no one is in a trance.

    (Creative closure: refer back to the intrigue)

Coel Coleman

THE DISTANCE COMMUNICATION PERFORMANCE AND RADIO/TV MEDIUMS

When you speak in front of any electronic device, you must be aware of the device without being obsessed with its presence. You may be able to see some of the audience members thru satellite or internet sites or you may be speaking on television where many audience members are not present.

    If you are speaking for a national or international conference with people at different site locations, or if you are speaking for the television audience, you can expect

the viewers to be extremely diverse in race, gender, education level, attitudes and beliefs.

Also, people tend to be more direct when they are not physically in your presence so be prepared for difficult questions or hostile audience members. Behind cameras and electronic devices, people are more bold and uninhibited.

Mediated communication can take place morning, noon or night. That is one of the core conveniences of technology. Because people in California can speak to people in New York without getting on an airplane, make sure that you are alert and prepared with your message regardless of the time of day set forth by the parties.

Be ready for a question and answer forum. First, paraphrase the question. Secondly, answer the question directly and quickly before trying to expound. If you don't know an answer, be honest and let the person asking the question know that you are unable to answer at that time. Reassure the person that you will have an answer after you investigate.

If you are at a satellite or internet conference, meeting or interview, do not play to the camera. Know your material well enough to look at the camera but don't be a character. Act natural and sincere while also being poised and engaging. You have to pretend the cameras are not there or you could appear over-animated and phony. Avoid too much movement and try to be as relaxed and as confident as possible.

If you are in front of a television camera or you know you are being tape-recorded, be extremely articulate and clear. Have good posture and look at the entire audience unless the only audience is the one watching on television. If that's the case, then look into the camera and speak as if the viewers are in the room with you. Don't get wide-eyed. Relax your body and your eyes.

Choose clothes that are slighty darker in hue. Don't wear all white; sometimes it causes a glare for the camera. Be careful of clothing patterns or colors that are distracting. Conservative colors and dress are best for any media influenced presentation.

If you are speaking for radio, your audience can only hear you so your voice must be varied and exciting. Stay about ten inches away from the microphone so there is little electronic feedback. Talk into the microphone! People often start talking and turning their heads to look around. If you do this, the audience can't hear you. Your mouth must be facing the microphone without putting your mouth on the microphone.

Suggested Aids

Use any visual aids that are necessary to validate or enhance the meaning of your message.

- Hold up pictures of the new building site or the new dogs that will be involved in the K-9 unit

- Show large colorful graphs of how productivity has increased and make sure all people at the satellite center can see the data

---

A SAMPLE MANUSCRIPT OUTLINE

for

The Distance Communication Performance and Radio/TV Mediums

(For a satellite conference meeting)

INTRODUCTION

I. You are not on vacation but at least today, you get to be with different people around the country . . . New York, can you see and hear me? Las Vegas, can you see and hear me? . . .
(Intrigue: emotional statement and do a sound-check at each site)

II. We'll spend our time together discussing some strategies to increase employee morale at each regional office. As the chairperson for this initiative, I have spent several months conducting interviews with staff members and reading surveys about weaknesses within our organization.
(Introduce the topic and tell why you are qualified to speak)

III. If productivity is low at one location, eventually the drop will affect all locations and that means each one of us will be affected.
(Explain the benefits of listening)

IV. Today, each location will give a report on morale based on your surveys and then we will make a list of possible strategies, narrow that list to our top three strategies that we will actually try to implement immediately; and finally, we will take a break before the keynote speaker for

Professor Patty Parish often engages in distance communication when she shares information with faculty members at other universities.

each site speaks on a topic to fit this year's theme: *Still Growing, Still Changing, Still Working Hard for Our Clients.*
(Preview the main points)

Connecting words or phrases: Let's start in the West and work our way across . . . Maxine in Denver has agreed to be our recorder-secretary; she'll make our lists large enough for all of us to see the complaints and the strategies.

BODY

I. Las Vegas, introduce your spokesperson and then tell us what you found out. Let's hold all questions until after the report is given.
(First report is given)

Connecting words or phrases: Thank you Dan . . . Are there any questions for Dan?

II. We will now hear from Denver . . . Allison you're on.
(Second report is given)

Connecting words or phrases: Thanks Allison . . . Raise your hand if you have a question and you'll be recognized.

III. It looks like I'm last.
    A. Here in New York, there are two key complaints from all employees in the organization.
        1. Number one, there's not enough vacation time for any employee but especially the first year employee.
        2. Number two, a thirty minute lunch is not enough time to unwind and then re-energize for the second half of the day.

Connecting words or phrases: Take a look at the list of complaints. Let's take a short break to think and have light discussions, before returning in order to list the strategies each location has developed. Take fifteen and then re-connect.

(INTERMISSION)

IV. Welcome back everyone . . . Las Vegas, did your team come up with suggestions for your employee complaints?
(First report is given)

Connecting words or phrases: Thank you Dan . . . We won't comment during this brainstorming session until all suggestions are listed.

V. Denver, do you have suggestions?
(Second report is given)

Connecting words or phrases: Thanks Allison . . .

VI. Here in New York, we came up with the following suggestions

    A. For vacation:

        1. Instead of no vacation time for first year employees, we could allow them to have an extended weekend once they have put ten months in.

        2. We can add an extra day to existing vacation days calling it an appreciation extension day.

    B. The thirty-minute lunch issue was also discussed.

        1. We are willing to extend the lunch break to an hour.

Connecting words or phrases: Let's have a discussion so we can narrow all of this into our top three concerns that we will try to address immediately at our respective locations.

(DISCUSSION)

Connecting words or phrases: We will start with Las Vegas and begin our round of keynote speakers. Dan, please introduce your speaker.

(KEYNOTE SPEAKERS)

CONCLUSION

    I. This has been a productive and inspirational conference.
    (Indicate the end)

    II. We will change lunch from 30 minutes to 60 minutes; we will give one more fifteen minute break in the afternoon; and we will give a monetary incentive for outstanding work instead of a plaque. We will also remember what each speaker shared about growing, changing and working hard for our clients.
    (Summarize your main points)

    III. Let's boost morale and we will boost productivity. Remember what Norman Vincent Peale said, "Begin where you are; begin now."
    (Creative closure: quotation)

Coel Coleman

 # THE EULOGY

There is usually joy for the homecoming of a soul or profound sadness for the loss of a loved one. Regardless, most want to listen to what you have to say about the deceased. The audience will probably be a diverse body of family and friends.

Most services for the departed will be late in the morning, early afternoon or evening. Attire should be appropriate and conservative. There is a trend to move away from black since some families see death as a celebration and homecoming with The Lord. As the speaker, you should consult the family and wear the color and style that compliments the ceremony. Coordinator of Domestic Graduate Recruitment Amber B. DuVentre, M.S., shares the eulogy she gave at her beloved grandmother's funeral. Ms. DuVentre has years of training in public address and has won numerous awards for presentational speaking. (Also see her manuscript outline for The Farewell).

Suggested Aids

A sentimental object introduced in the beginning or at the end of the presentation, would be captivating.

- A stuffed animal the deceased always kept

- Sports memorabilia that was special

- A picture of the family

- A slide show of memorable moments with soft music in the background

---

A SAMPLE MANUSCRIPT OUTLINE

for

The Eulogy

INTRODUCTION

I. Psalm 118:24 of the Holy Bible reads, "This is the day that the Lord hath made, let us rejoice and be glad in it. I will say that again, "This is the day that the Lord hath made, let us rejoice and be glad in it!"
(Intrigue: quotation)

II. We have heard about Helen Cotton, her work in the community, in the church, and at the hospital. Everything that everyone has mentioned . . . is her. She loved the Lord, her family, and that hospital. She was proud of her work and she shared the joy of everyone's honors and awards, especially her children and grandchildren. But I want to tell you of Helen Cotton, as my grandmother!

(Introduce the topic and tell why you are qualified to speak)

III. To *truly* know her, was to love her because she was goodness and she trusted God's signs.

(Preview the main points)

Connecting words or phrases: Grandmother knew about goodness!

BODY

I. Psalm 23 reads, "Surely goodness and love will follow me all the days of my life, and I will dwell in the house of the LORD forever."

  A. She made everyone feel good with her kind words. She often said, "That is a nice suit! Was it on sale? I can't wear that now but put it upstairs with my good stuff." Or she would say, "No I don't want to put that on . . . that's my good dress."

  B. Also, she always had a compliment for everyone. Whether it was one's appearance, ability to do one's job, or one's cooking skills, she was always there to give an encouraging word.

  C. This encouragement was usually followed by questions or statements such as, "Why didn't you buy me one like it?" Or she would say, "Nobody takes care of me like you."

  D. See, she knew of the Lord's goodness.

  (First main point with support)

Connecting words or phrases: She also had a habit of asking us if the sign was right for us to do something.

  II. For anyone who doesn't know what I am speaking of, at the beginning of the New Year she always had to read a Farmer's Almanac and a Bible.

  A. It didn't matter what we had to do, from getting my ear's pierced, Phillip getting his wisdom teeth pulled, or Pierre having to drive back to college; she would ask, "Is the sign right?" She loved that Farmers Almanac and she loved the Bible. Both provided signs that she followed, as she lived her life.

B. Ecclesiastes 3:1, tells us that, "To everything there is a season, and a time to every purpose under the heaven." God knows our purpose, and He knew hers. He gave her signs.
(Second main point with support)

CONCLUSION

I. I share all of this with you today, because I believe that on Tuesday, November 6th, at 11:00 P.M., the Lord looked at His book and knew that He let us borrow His "good stuff" . . . our mother . . . our grandmother . . . our friend.
(Indicate the end and summarize your main points)

II. And on that Tuesday, He said, "Well done, Helen Cotton, thou good and faithful servant, the sign is right for you . . . to come home!
(Creative closure: emotional statement)

Manuscript outline submitted by:
Amber B. DuVentre, M.S.
Coordinator of Domestic Graduate Recruitment
Murray State University

THE FAREWELL

There are mixed emotions when you say goodbye. When you say farewell in a public place, people expect you to be a little sad about leaving and a little excited about your new venture. Therefore, you don't want to antagonize your audience with "good riddens" facial expressions and body language. Be honest and sincere but also have class and be gracious. Thank anyone who helped you to succeed at the place you're leaving while showing genuine enthusiasm for your new endeavor.

Farewell presentations are often part of an entire program that includes food, speakers and other activities. Be brief; and humor is encouraged as long as it's tasteful.

Communication and recruitment expert Amber B. DuVentre gave this farewell presentation when she was promoted in her career. (Also, see her manuscript outline for The Eulogy).

Suggested Aids

Presentation aids are really not needed for this short presentation. The power is in the emotion you show when saying goodbye. However, you could try:

- Party-type objects thrown into the air at the end of the presentation

- A picture of you and your co-workers

A SAMPLE MANUSCRIPT OUTLINE
for
The Farewell

INTRODUCTION

I. Confucius once said, "The mechanic that would perfect his work must first sharpen his tools."
(Intrigue: quotation)

II. I'm sure that when I pack my things to leave this office, the toolbox that I brought with me will be a little heavier.
(Introduce the topic)

III. I have been able to improve my knowledge of the university, while meeting some great individuals along the way.
(Preview the main points)

Connecting words or phrases: I've learned so much about this institution.

BODY

I. Who knows that Lovett Auditorium used to be the old basketball arena? Who knows that the footbridge is where an actual street use to be? Who knows that the original Racer One, *Violet Rose,* is buried in a corner of Stewart Stadium?

    A. After working for the School Relations Office, I know these things! Having a passion for this university is necessary if you recruit, but knowing about the little things that make Murray unique is what makes my departure bittersweet.

    B. I have learned so many facets about higher education and even more about this university. I now appreciate its history and its legacy.
    (First main point with support)

Connecting words or phrases: Although random facts are important, nothing compares to the people who I have had the pleasure to work with during this time.

II. I know that we can all share stories about prospective students and their visits to our university. However, we all know that nothing compares to going to work and loving the people you work with each day.

    A. I will always remember the students that I have recruited and the relationships that I have built. They are priceless; and so are the memories that I have from working with this wonderful staff.

    B. To the administration of this division, thank you again for the professional and personal development opportunities that you gave me over the last six years, as a student and as an employee. This office has been a place where I felt that I could grow, learn, and succeed.

C. Because of the knowledge and skills that I have acquired, my career has taken a different direction and I feel it is time to move on to new opportunities and challenges. I have accepted a position in the Provost's Office, as the Coordinator of Graduate Recruitment.

(Second main point with support)

CONCLUSION

I. Now, as I leave, I take inventory of the tools in my box to see if I have what I need to be effective.

(Indicate the end)

II. My knowledge and friendships are cherished as I pack the following tools ...

(Summarize your main points)

III. There's a hard hat-to protect the knowledge that I have gained. There's a hammer to pound out the details of necessary information that I will need to succeed. I found a screwdriver to make sure the detailed information is connected tightly; lastly, I have a ruler. I have something to use to measure the exceptional work that I plan to do ... with what I have learned ... from this great office.

(Creative closures: emotional statements)

Manuscript outline submitted by:
Amber B. DuVentre, M.S.
Coordinator of Domestic Graduate Recruitment
Murray State University

 **The Fundraising/Charity Address**

The speaker for a fundraising or charity address is just as important as the actual presentation. It is important for you to remember that as the chosen speaker, the organization is trusting you will make an address that will be interesting, timely, moving, and appropriate. The focus of the evening is the charity and the goal is for you to enhance the evening with an address that will assist with fundraising efforts as well as making the event a positive and memorable experience for the attendees.

Gather information about the charity or organization to ensure that you will be able to provide a strong address that will assist in the fundraising goals. Below are several tips to consider when preparing and delivering a fundraising/charity address:

- Research the organization to learn its mission and service(s) provided to the community
  - Include the organization's mission in your address
- Ask the organization's representative:
  - about the history of the event and what the organization hopes to accomplish by having the event
  - if the event is black tie, after five, or casual, so your attire is appropriate
  - what theme or particular topic is being embraced by the organization
  - about the time frame for your address
  - about the donors and clients who may be in attendance
- Tie in heart-warming stories or examples that will be relevant to the evening's purpose and that will stir audience emotions
- Allow yourself adequate time to draft an address that has a clear introduction, body, and conclusion
  - After you intrigue the audience, thank the organization and its leadership for allowing you the opportunity and honor to speak
  - Focus your address on the theme or a specific topic (i.e., persistence, reaching goals, strength)
  - Personalize the address so attendees feel like you are connected to the organization or the cause
  - Include humor where appropriate to maintain the audience's attention; and include humor to assist you with building a rapport with the audience
  - Share why this organization was worth your time
  - It is a good idea to conclude your address with a brief story (less than 45 seconds) that illustrates the point of your message. The story should be poignant and leave the listeners with a message that will remain with them after the evening has ended
  - Stay within your time-frame
- After the initial draft, allow yourself a day to step away from the address and revisit it at another time; read it aloud with fresh eyes and ears
- Ask friends and colleagues to read and listen to the address to help identify inconsistencies or unclear sections

Catherine Cushinberry, Ph.D.
Executive Director
Boys and Girls Club of Jackson-Madison County, TN
Adjunct Professor at Union University

People are in your presence because they care about the cause. However, they also want to be validated and assured that their money won't be wasted. Usually, this presentation is also an after-dinner speech. There may be a cocktail reception or banquet. The attendees may have paid for their meal with the proceeds going to the nonprofit organization.

Microphones are a must! Wear a lavaliere microphone even if you have a podium/lectern because this way you can walk around and not be stuck behind the podium. You will need to be extremely sincere and passionate. You need to believe in the cause you claim to be supporting. You need to practice what you preach and *you* should give a donation.

Be well rehearsed. Dress for the occasion and make sure nothing you wear is distracting. Memorize the introduction and conclusion. Be convincing and people will donate. Be sincere and they will donate more than they had originally planned to donate. Be convincing, sincere and well-spoken and you will be the catalyst for a Capital Campaign goal exceeding the expectation.

Suggested Aids

Any aid is appropriate if it solidifies your message.

- Holding up a dollar bill is effective and actually handing money to someone in the audience to show "generosity" is always a crowd pleaser

- Giving a small object like a gold coin with the date and the theme of the affair on it would be a nice presentation aid and gift

- A clip showing a sad scene depicting the need for funds is effective at a fundraiser; however, make sure it's not too graphic or emotional

---

A SAMPLE MANUSCRIPT OUTLINE
for
The Fundraising/Charity Address

INTRODUCTION

I. I started to write a speech but then I stopped. I started to write something that would inspire someone ... but then I stopped ... I started to prepare some words for you so that you would donate money to Julia's House ... this beautiful place filled with faces of people who got away from their abusers but who still live in fear. I started to write a speech but then I stopped.
(Intrigue: emotional statements)

II. Every second of every day . . . someone stops. I know abused men and women who are afraid to pick up a phone and call for help. You know a victim too . . . even if you can't think of a name.
   (Introduce the topic and tell why you are qualified to speak)

III. Victims are at your jobs and within your families . . . You know the victim . . . the student who is raped by an uncle who insists she gave him a secret signal that she wanted him . . . the co-worker who makes the best coffee and smiles at you everyday . . . the male college student abused physically and emotionally by his girlfriend but who knows that everyone has problems in a relationship and he IS lucky to have her . . . the person who speaks at fundraisers . . . Hmm.
   (Explain the benefits of listening)

IV. But three things are clear to me: Someone always stops; stopping gives power to the abuser, and fear imprisons freedom.
   (Preview the main points)

Connecting words or phrases: Someone stops.

BODY
I. Someone always stops.
   A. Stops calling the police . . . stops telling friends . . . stops filing that restraining order.
      1. According to The Bureau of Justice Statistics accessed on July 10, 2008, although more people are reporting abuse, many do not. Sixty percent of men and women fail to report abuse because they feel nothing will be done. Twenty percent of male and female victims are afraid their abusers will retaliate if they report the abuse. (fictitious organization and citation)
   B. Stopping is also expensive.
      1. Julia's House costs thousands of dollars to maintain. Shelters like Julia's require all the essential elements to help victims live in a decent environment from providing food to paying for caseworkers. Donations are given but like everything else, there's never enough money to support all of the needs that need to be met. It is such a shame that the victims can't go home.
      2. Instead they are compelled to go to a strange house named after a person they are not related to and sleep in a decent environment but certainly not their home.
      (First main point with support)

Connecting words or phrases: The abuser?

II. Well, every time we stop, we allow that person to rape, abuse and kill all over again.
   A. The miracle of living free from fear, self-hate, depression, pain, dependency, humiliation and isolation is lost when we stop.

1. According to Pennsylvania's Office for Stopping Violence website accessed July 12, 2008, many men say that they would not have gone to a batterer program if they had not been court ordered to do so. Some go as a way to convince their partners not to leave them. Unless a batterer is truly committed to being accountable for his or her behavior and to stop being controlling, he or she is unlikely to change the abusive behavior. (fictitious organization and citation)

   2. Also, many abusers have been abused by someone so they rarely feel bad for anyone but themselves. They see themselves as the victims. So, when someone stops, power is given to the guilty.

   B. Let's call her Mrs. X. She did call the police after he burned her with his cigarette in front of her thirteen year-old son.

   1. She did file a restraining order after he banged her head into the wall but still said it was her fault because she made him angry . . . He felt that her crying after he called her lazy and ugly, was dramatic and uncalled for.

   2. Guess what? She even made it to her brother's house . . . but after a week and numerous phone calls . . . she stopped. She went home . . . We buried her this year.
   (Second main point with support)

Connecting words or phrases: She's free now . . . but we're not.

III. Until we are no longer afraid to tell our uncle, sorority sister, mother, teacher, father, teammate, and friend that their abuse of another person is wrong, we can't be free.

   A. It's scary, but until we are willing to risk being ignored in our communities, talked about at work, ex-communicated by our families, dumped by our friends, we can not be free.

   1. We are imprisoned by our own fear to get help and our fear to expose a perpetrator. It shows how fear sometimes has a greater impact than the act itself.

   B. It's scary, but until we admit that there are more victims than we pretend there are . . . we can not be free.

   1. We spend so much time with phony public relations. We want to appear perfect. We want for our families to appear successful at home and at work. We want to appear so wonderful that we neglect our health and our ability to be happy for the sake of "appearing" happy.
   (Third main point with support)

CONCLUSION

I. Today, I started to write a speech but then I stopped.
(Indicate the end)

II. So, I challenge each one in this room to finish my speech. To pick up where I left off. To give to those who need us . . . those who stopped . . . those who don't realize the abuser won't stop . . . those who live in a prison of fear.

(Summarize your main points)

III. Everyone in this room can't stop. Men and women have to work together. We can't afford to stop. Don't stop donating your money to places like Julia's House. Don't stop educating, fighting and loving yourselves. Don't stop praying and believing that life can be wonderful. Don't stop . . . before this message becomes a miracle.

(Creative closures: emotional statements)

Coel Coleman

THE HOLIDAY CELEBRATION

Celebrations are usually fun for most who attend them. Alcohol and food are often provided. Be aware of the atmosphere. Many do not want to hear long speeches but rather brief moments of reflection for the period of time that's being celebrated. Brevity is so important if you want your audience to really listen to your message.

Image © U.P. images_vector, 2009. Used under license from Shutterstock, Inc.

The formality will dictate the use of humor and the length of the presentation. The more formal the celebration, the longer the presentation can be and the more humor should be regulated. During your presentation, make sure you recognize the holiday and say a few words about the occasion. Rehearse this presentation. It's short but it's still a presentation.

Agnes C. DuVentre gives you an example of a presentation for a holiday celebration. She's been an educator, administrator and motivational speaker for over 30 years.

Suggested Aids

Aids are not needed but some possibilities are:

- A slide show of organization members
- A raised glass of champagne or sparkling cider to toast the guests
- Holiday objects you can pass out for the audience members to keep

A SAMPLE MANUSCRIPT OUTLINE

for

The Holiday Celebration

INTRODUCTION

   I. School Board members, our fine principal Dr. Williams, faculty, staff, parents, and students, as we gather here for this Thanksgiving Brunch, let us not forget the words of Miester Echkart who wrote, "If the only prayer you said in your whole life was, 'thank you,' that would suffice."
   (Intrigue: quotation)

   II. So on this Saturday afternoon before Thanksgiving Day, we say, "THANK YOU."
   (Introduce the topic)

   III. We are so delighted that you've taken the time to let us treat you to this well-deserved luncheon that was prepared by our Teen Living class. These students have been training all year to host these functions. I love being a part of this class!
   (Tell why you are qualified to speak)

   IV. But, before we dine, let's talk a little about this celebration because Thanksgiving Day is about family, fun, and food.
   (Preview the main points)

BODY

   I. As most of us know, the middle school years are difficult for everyone.
   A. As a student, you are transitioning out of elementary school and leaving friends; parents are dealing with budding personalities; and educators are picking up the pieces from both the students and the parents. Here at Northeast Middle School, we pride ourselves in creating a family type atmosphere for our students.
      1. So, on their triumphs we encourage, on their failed attempts we build up, and on their hard work and achievements we celebrate as a family.
      2. From the Teen Living family, we invite you to make yourselves at home.

Connecting words or phrases: We want you to be comfortable and we want you to have fun!

   II. We could more than likely all agree that from the time we were little, we were told not to play with our food.
   A. Well here in the Teen Living class, we feel that playing and having fun is a part of learning. No mom and dad, we don't let them play with their food, but we do encourage them to observe *you* while you cook.

B. Teens learn so much from their guardians. We hope they have fun and foster a healthy lifestyle while learning new things. I believe that everyone here understands that fun is an important part of learning and getting an education.

Connecting words or phrases: However, there is one more element of Thanksgiving.

III. Although the young men are really shy at first about cooking, after getting started, they love it.

    A. As you might imagine, cooking with these students is fun. As the parents can share with you, some them have never been in the kitchen other than to eat, so this is a neat experience for them to have.

    B. Because they prepare these dishes as a part of their assignments, and because they are so eager to learn to cook, they take great pride in the food that you see before you. All of the students were eager to cook for you. A lot of love went into this meal.

CONCLUSION

I. As we prepare to dine, we thank each one of you for your presence today and your support throughout the year.
(Indicate the end)

II. I hope to hear more laughter during this day of family, fun and food.
(Summarize your main points)

III. Poet Jack Prelutsy says it best in his poem "Ate Too Much Turkey."

<blockquote>
I ate too much turkey; I ate too much corn,
I ate too much pudding and pie,
I'm stuffed up with muffins and much too much stuffin',
I'm probably going to die.
I piled up my plate and I ate and I ate,
But I wish I had known when to stop,
For I'm so crammed with yams, sauces, gravies, and jams
That my buttons are starting to pop.
I'm full of tomatoes and french fried potatoes,
My stomach is swollen and sore,
But there's still some dessert, so I guess it won't hurt
if I eat just a little bit more.
</blockquote>

Text copyright © 1982 by Jack Prelutsky

(Creative closure: long quotation)

Manuscript outline submitted by:
Agnes C. DuVentre
Instructor of Family & Consumer Science
Jackson- Madison County School System (TN)

THE INFORMATIVE LECTURE OR KEYNOTE ADDRESS

People are diverse! We all have different experiences. In a class setting, the majority of students want to learn but they also want to get good grades that will help them to get good jobs. In a work environment, the employees and employers want to learn so their earning potential increases. Either way, the listeners at a lecture usually want to understand and retain your message. As a speaker, be ready for outside noise and inner nervousness. Also, you could get horrible nonverbals from the audience members! Be prepared for anything and don't be distracted!

As a featured presenter, you should have prolonged periods of eye contact, and controlled gestures.

Image © Tony Wear, 2009. Used under license from Shutterstock, Inc.

Lectures are basic in form and in delivery. You must try to practice with some type of recording device. Students are usually apathetic about classroom lectures so you MUST be exciting when you deliver this type of presentation. Employees and employers are less apathetic but if you are dull, then the purpose of the presentation is lost. You need to make sure you raise and lower the pitch of your voice. Show emotional levels through your facial expressions.

In the following sample manuscript outline by student Emma L. Millman, there is information about the *No Child Left Behind Act.* If you were to deliver this speech, your facial expressions should convey enthusiasm about the Act but also disgust for children who are neglected. Your face should reflect your words.

Suggested Aids

Any visual aid that will excite and motivate the audience to listen will be appropriate. For the following speech:

- A very large 20×28 picture of a child left alone would be good to show how children are left behind

- A dollar bill explaining how more money is needed for education

- A graph of statistics of how education has improved with this Act

A SAMPLE MANUSCRIPT OUTLINE
for
The Informative Lecture or Keynote Address

INTRODUCTION

I. Sixty-four percent of the nation's fourth graders cannot solve 2001 minus 25. Yes, sixty-four percent.
(Intrigue: emotional statements)

II. According to a report by the U.S. Department of Education on February 10, 2004, math education is not up to par with today's global needs.
(Introduce the topic and tell why the audience should listen)

III. As a future high school math teacher, I will be held accountable for teaching students as directed by the *No Child Left Behind Act,* known as the NCLB.
(Tell why you are qualified to speak)

IV. The NCLB addresses issues such as accountability, teacher quality and incentives for achievement, especially within the area of math.
(Preview the main points)

Connecting words or phrases: The NCLB holds schools accountable for every student's education.

BODY

I. One of the goals of the NCLB is to make sure that schools are teaching what needs to be taught, including the basics like math.
    A. Accountability is measured through yearly testing.
        1. Over the past few years, test scores have been rising slowly. According to the *U.S. News* on September 26, 2007, some credit belongs to the NCLB.
        2. An education think tank noted that the NCLB does not deserve full credit since there has been improvement pre-dating it.
    B. Regardless, measurements are in place and math is emphasized in the curriculum.
        1. President Bush, in Maria Glod's article in the *Washington Post* on December 5, 2007, stated that focusing on the basics will improve math education.
        2. However, the NCLB does leave some holes in the math curriculum. By focusing so heavily on what is tested, students are denied a full math education, according to Gordon Cawelti's article in *Educational Leadership* in November 2006.
        (First main point with support)

Connecting words or phrases: In order to meet the standards, more qualified teachers are in demand.

    II. The NCLB policy states that highly qualified teachers are required in order to effectively improve education.
        A. These teachers would be the basis for accountability.
            1. In the NCLB's Proven Methods section on September 15, 2004, the government advocates improving and expanding the training of math teachers.
            2. Although this strengthens teachers, some feel it also creates more hoops for them to jump through, according to a student in the Murray State University Education Department in a face-to-face 2008 interview.
        B. In addition to accountability, qualified teachers must also have a strong drive.
            1. The Proven Methods section reflects a teacher's responsibility in a student's education through testing. This is an effective means for teachers to evaluate their teaching.
            2. However, according to Cawelti, a teacher's effectiveness being determined by testing is negatively affecting teacher morale.
        (Second main point with support)

Connecting words or phrases: However, there are incentives offered by the NCLB to help increase teacher morale.

    III. In order to encourage schools to produce positive results, the NCLB offers states and teachers additional funding.
        A. The NCLB offers rewards for states that demonstrate rising achievement.
            1. Schools that make improvements receive more federal grants.
            2. However, if schools do not improve, they risk losing federal funding.
        B. The NCLB also offers monetary rewards for teachers for rising achievements.
            1. Overall, Proven Methods would increase the pay for math and science teachers. But according to the *U.S. News* on November 2, 2007, the National Education Association believes that this is unfair to other teachers.
            2. Teachers with students who show exceptional progress are also rewarded with bonuses. However, this is based on test scores alone. This seems unfair to some teachers.
        (Third main point with support)

Connecting words or phrases: The NCLB is a piece of federal legislation designed to improve academics. Some think the legislation is fair; some do not. It's value appears to be subjective.

CONCLUSION
    I. We are in a period of educational reform.
    (Indicate the end)

II. The NCLB addresses accountability, teacher quality and it offers incentives to promote improvement in academics, with math as one of its main focuses.

(Summarize your main points)

III. With measures in place, perhaps one day, all students will be able to solve 2001 minus 25; but in the meantime, as the great mathematical expositor Paul Halmos said, "The only way to learn mathematics is to do mathematics."

(Creative closures: refer back to the intrigue and a quotation)

Manuscript outline submitted by:
Emma L. Millman
Secondary Education Major
Mathematics Area
Murray State University

THE INTERVIEW

There are so many reasons why you may be an interviewer or an interviewee. Whether you are student, a person with an established career or a job applicant, knowing how to ask and answer questions with poise, enthusiasm and organized thoughts in an interview situation, is paramount. Although the role of the interviewer is explored, the focus of this section is on the interviewee and how he or she can become a strong candidate for employment.

DeChelle L. Forbes, M.A., Rector/Assistant Dean for the Honors College at Coppin State University in Baltimore, Maryland, has been an educator and administrator for years. She has taught communication skills including interviewing. She shares her insight and her example of a mock interview for a student internship with tips included. She also gives some closing comments.

 Preparing for the Interview

Today's scholar knows that a professionally charged resume can propel him/her to the front of the line of recent graduates. Anyone pursuing a career goal knows the importance of a resume. The key to such a resume will depend upon your ability to persuade an employer that your raw talent and initiative can translate into productivity. Such persuasion takes place in the interview. The interview is your opportunity to sell your strengths, abilities, and skills. In a word, succeeding in the interview requires *preparation,* the best anecdote for fear. Preparation requires research of the two main players in the interview process: the employer and you.

The Employer

An employer wants to know what you will contribute to the organization. Are you simply interested in the pay, or will you adopt for yourself the mission of the organization? Therefore, gather key facts about the company and include its history, its corporate structure and climate, its most recent products or marketing strategies, its viability within the industry, its presence in the community, etc.

Be able to demonstrate how you believe you will fit into the company. The facts you uncover will prompt questions that you will ask at the conclusion of the interview. You should also become familiar with questions an employer may pose, and prepare your answers as a part of your preparation.

Get help from career service experts so that you are prepared for your interview.

You

In the interview, you are the product that you must market. Who knows you better than you? Take some time to identify your transferable skills that you have developed over the course of time in class, in leadership positions, or at that part-time job. Figure out what skills will transfer from your experiences to a new position.

So, research yourself. Consider your most-liked courses, your least-liked courses, and the skills that come easily to you. Think about and formulate your short-term and long-term professional goals and your plans to accomplish them. Your research is complete when you can answer with ease, "Why should we hire you?" and "Tell us about yourself." Both of these questions seek information about your accomplishments and career goals.

Practice, Proper Attire, and Overall Conduct at the Interview

Practice is important for gaining confidence and becoming comfortable with the interview process whether you are the interviewer or the interviewee. You can practice with a friend or request a mock interview with a campus career development office. Absorb the constructive criticism and make necessary adjustments. Practice with a recorder and rate your vocal quality. Are you too shrill? Do you speak too rapidly? Are there too many extraneous or filler words (uh, um, right, you know) in your speech? Practice in front of a mirror, or, if possible, videotape yourself. Does your body language reveal rigidity or nervousness?

When it comes to attire, the adage that clothes make the man or woman is particularly true in the interview process. You will be rated on your appearance so make an investment in a matching, conservative suit of good quality. Accessories should be minimal to include perfume or cologne. A quality ink pen and a portfolio stuffed with hard or electronic copies (CD or flash drive) of your resume are a must.

Your overall conduct will also be heavily measured. If you are the interviewee, plan to arrive at least fifteen minutes before the interview. Of course, if you are the interviewer, you have more power to be late; but if you are disrespectful with time, a great applicant may not want to work for you!

Everyone involved should have good eye contact, a warm smile, and a good handshake. These things are remembered. Maintain eye contact and nod sparingly to indicate receptiveness. Do blink occasionally. Staring is rude and incessant nodding may indicate a deeper problem. ☺ A warm smile is engaging and a firm—not painful—handshake should begin and end the interview.

Suggested Aids

- A clean copy of your resume, cover letter and reference sheet

- A sample of your writing skills

- An object that you made that reflects your ability

A SAMPLE MANUSCRIPT
for
The Interview

(For a student internship)

(Arrive 15 minutes early. Disable cell phone.)

INTERVIEWER: *Please tell me about yourself.*

TIP: Limit your answer to your major field of study and your career goals.

APPLICANT: I became interested in the media while in high school. I got started by being a part of the camera crew that filmed the athletic games, and I fell in love with production. I then, tried my hand at anchoring our school's news and realized that I wanted to major in mass media in college. In both my freshman and sophomore years of college, I became a member of the newspaper and yearbook staffs and I have my own campus radio program. However, I believe my niche is in media production. My goal is to one day own my own media production company.

Make sure your eye contact and posture reflect confidence and desire to work for that organization.

INTERVIEWER: *Why should I hire you?*

TIP: This question could make or break the interview. Use your experience gained in paid and non-paid positions, your extra-curricular activities, coursework, and initiative to show yourself as the most qualified and capable candidate. Be sure to make a clear transfer of skills to the job opening.

APPLICANT: I understand that the Media Production Intern position requires a major in communications in addition to excellent writing skills, exposure to studio production, and demonstrated evidence of creativity. Although I do not have extensive experience in the field, I do bring to XYZ Incorporated and to the position, job-related, hands-on experience from the classroom and from my extra-curricular activities. In my studio production course, I was required to work with two other students to create a music video using a combination of photography, audio technology and television camera techniques. I was involved in every aspect of the production and received an "A" for the project. I would like to leave a DVD of the production for your review.

As I mentioned earlier, I've also worked on every aspect of the compilation of the yearbook to include its design, photography, and caption writing for the last two years. If needed, I believe I could also serve as voice-over talent for any production; I believe I've enhanced my speaking skills as a member of the campus radio's on-air staff.

I believe these skills, coupled with a lot of initiative, mirror the requirements of the position and I would well-serve XYZ.

INTERVIEWER: *What are your career goals? Where do you see yourself in five years?*

TIP: Your career goals should be modified to fit your career intentions at the time. For instance, it is okay to mention that you would like to own your own media production company when interviewing for an internship position. However, to mention it in an interview for a permanent position may disqualify you from consideration because it would raise concern about your longevity with the company.

APPLICANT: At the moment, my goal is to gain as much experience in the field as possible. In such a field, I understand that I must be willing to begin at the ground level. Immediately following college, I am willing to begin my career as a production assistant. I plan to learn as much as I can about every aspect of the profession and then in five years, I envision myself starting my own production company.

INTERVIEWER: *What do you consider your strengths?*

TIP: Offer strengths that will compliment the position you are seeking, and offer short examples from your work experience and extra-curricular activities to support them. Do not oversell. Overselling your skills may prompt the employer to poke holes in your confidence.

APPLICANT: I believe that my strength is my ability to envision the finished product. With the project that I mentioned earlier, I was very meticulous in the piecing together of the project as I understand that quality is in the details. I also believe that I have learned the art of multi-tasking as I handle the demands of my academic program, my extra-curricular activities, and a part-time job; and yet, I have been able to maintain a 3.5 grade point average.

INTERVIEWER: *That's impressive; but everyone has a weakness. What is your greatest weakness?*

TIP: The trick is to turn your weakness into something that will benefit the employer. Never offer a true weakness such as, "I have difficulty making it to class on time." However, an obvious, understandable weakness is acceptable. The following statement is a weakness but it also has elements of strength that will benefit the employer.

APPLICANT: There are times when I take on more responsibility than I can handle. I have a difficult time saying "no" when something needs to be done, even if it's not my primary responsibility and I am busy with my own work. Another weakness is that while I have a lot of initiative and education, I do lack some career-related experience, as my resume suggests. (This is an example of an obvious, understandable weakness.)

INTERVIEWER: *What is your favorite course? What is your least favorite course? Why?*

TIP: Your answers should relate to your career aspirations.

APPLICANT: My favorite course is most definitely Introduction to Media Production. I enjoy this course because it has provided me an overview of my favorite aspect of the media, and it has enhanced skills that I developed in high school. My least favorite course, so far, has been Calculus. I actually performed well in the course, but I tend to be more excited about courses in which I can use skills that directly relate to my major such as writing, public speaking, and publication design.

INTERVIEWER: *How do you handle stress?*

TIP: Prove to the interviewer that you are well-rounded and that you have an outlet for stress. This is the opportunity to share your involvement in extra-curricular activities as well.

APPLICANT: I have been able to juggle classes as well as leadership positions in a few campus organizations. My membership in the Photography Club has been most rewarding because I love the hobby, and I find it very relaxing. I'm also a member of the Running Club which allows me to "download," so to speak, the day's activities and any stressors I might have encountered.

INTERVIEWER: *What do you know about our company?*

TIP: Demonstrate your interest in the organization by researching the company using the company's website or industry/trade journals.

APPLICANT: In addition to the internship opportunity offered at XYZ, I was excited about the possibility of working in one of the fastest growing production companies in the state of Maryland. In fact, I learned that it is the second largest production company, responsible for a large number of advertising campaigns in the tri-state area. Also, I served as a volunteer with the Women's Homeless Shelter, and I am glad to see that XYZ is a company sponsor.

INTERVIEWER: *Do you have any questions for me?*

The interviewer will always give you an opportunity to ask questions. As a rule, always ask at least two questions at the conclusion of the interview. As mentioned earlier, your research will give rise to some questions. Others will be prompted simply by your interest in the position. Please note that failure to ask questions may indicate indifference towards the organization or position.

10 Questions You Could Ask at an Interview

1. What is a typical day like as an intern?
2. Would you describe the assignments given to the media intern?
3. What skills are absolutely necessary to be successful in this position?
4. To whom would the media intern report?
5. Is there a formal training period, or am I expected to shadow a staff member?
6. What is considered a typical work week? Is overtime ever required?
7. How and when can I expect to be evaluated?
8. Is there the possibility of employment extending beyond the scheduled internship time period?
9. When should I expect a decision regarding my application?
10. If selected, when can I expect to begin?

Questions You Should *Not* Ask at an Interview

- What does your company do?
- Can you give me your opinion of my interview?
- How much can I expect to make per week?
- Will there be any opportunity to take a vacation?
- I have a morning class; would I be able to alter my internship schedule to accommodate it?

The appropriate time to ask these questions is after you have been offered the position.

Don't forget the "thank you letter." It serves two purposes and should always follow the interview. Obviously, the thank you letter expresses gratitude for the employer's time. The interview is a privilege, not a right. However, the letter also provides yet another opportunity to sell yourself to the interviewer by re-stating an important point that you made in the interview, and it will assist him or her in remembering you. Failure to send the thank you letter could eliminate you from consideration.

Preparation for any interview is a job in itself, and as with any job, it requires hard work. However, it also comes with certain perks: a thorough understanding of all that you have to offer, increased confidence, and of course, the possibility of the perfect job or career.

Interview tips, manuscript, and questions submitted by:
DeChelle L. Forbes, M.A.
Rector/Assistant Dean
Honors College
Coppin State University

THE INTRODUCTION OF A KEYNOTE SPEAKER

Either you know this person or you don't. If you know the person, you will only need to confirm important background information. Make sure you don't include personal information that could be embarrassing. It may be funny that you saw him trip over a cat; but that is not appropriate information to share with an audience. Don't make the speaker look or feel silly. If you don't know the speaker, make sure you have the correct pronunciation of the name, company, job title, etc.

There is nothing worse than having someone introduce a speaker incorrectly. Giving wrong data about a person will upset most keynote speakers and cause them to lose focus on their presentation. He or she will usually speak out and correct the person introducing him or her. This will cause both parties to be embarrassed and you will look incompetent and unprepared. Your job is to make the speaker sound so interesting that people will be eager to hear what he or she has to say!

Since this is such a short presentation, you should be very familiar with your presentation and completely engaging! If you are reading off a piece of paper and not

Image © JupiterImages Corp., 2009.

having eye contact, you will not create interest for the upcoming speaker. It's your job to make the audience want to listen to the speaker. The introduction can create anticipation or fall flat and force the speaker to create his or her own enthusiasm, thus putting the speaker in a position where he or she has to be great just to counter your lackluster performance.

Suggested Aids

- Show a large picture of the keynote speaker
- Show an object that represents that person's wonderful personality or achievement to stimulate interest in the keynote speaker

---

A SAMPLE MANUSCRIPT OUTLINE
for
The Introduction of a Keynote Speaker

(All references and names are fictitious)

INTRODUCTION

  I. Many have seen her but few have heard her words of wisdom.
  (Intrigue: emotional statement)

  II. She's here to share her dream for your future. It is a privilege to introduce someone I've known for over ten years.
  (Introduce the topic and tell why you are qualified to speak)

  III. Her experiences can help all of us learn the benefits of giving back to our communities.
  (Explain the benefits of listening)

  IV. Her contributions to education and to the well-being of our children are too numerous to mention. From her work with the Big Brother/Big Sister program, to her mission work overseas, she has been the rock that many have leaned upon.
  (Preview the main points)

Connecting words or phrases: She has been with Big Brothers/Big Sisters for 20 years.

BODY

  I. Within this wonderful organization, she has served as a Big Sister, area coordinator and then as the director of one of the largest offices in the United States.

   A. In 2008, it was documented in the August 12th edition of *Best Leaders Magazine* that under her leadership, the membership doubled and the donations tripled.

Her vision led to more regional and national participation from celebrities and dignitaries.

(First main point with support)

Connecting words or phrases: However, her work is not limited to our great country.

II. She is selfless. She shares her time and strength with people in smaller countries. As a missionary, she has traveled to Mexico, Africa and even the Middle East helping to build homes, schools and positive relationships.

    A. Tonight, she will show a few slides of her most memorable experiences and allow each one of us to know just how blessed we are to have so many basic needs that we often take for granted.

    (Second main point with support)

CONCLUSION

I. I just don't have the time to tell you how many lives have been enriched through her service.

(Indicate the end)

II. Her work with Big Brothers and Big Sisters of America and her work as a missionary have expanded her knowledge and her passion for empowering humankind.

(Summarize your main points)

III. Lori Kim Marks is more than a woman of accomplishments; she's a woman of miracles. I present to you, Mrs. Lori ... Kim ... Marks!

(Creative closure: emotional statement)

Coel Coleman

 # THE MASTER OR MISTRESS OF CEREMONIES

Most people want to be at an event that requires a Master or Mistress of Ceremonies. Regardless of the formality, people want to feel appreciated for attending. If the audience is made up of children, adults, or both, the Master or Mistress of Ceremonies sets the tone for the entire event. If you don't make people feel happy to be there, they won't get the maximum joy for attending that event. You must be organized and energetic for the crowd to respond favorably before, during and after the event.

Most formal or informal events are in the late afternoon or evening. Flashy attire can work for this type of presentation because you are the first and last person the audience will see. Exciting attire will actually excite the audience and make people aware of the magnitude of the event. "Flashy and exciting" do not mean tacky. Too much flesh showing or too many wardrobe distractions can take away from the keynote speaker or activities. You want to enhance the event with your presence not serve as a solo act.

The master/mistress of ceremonies should display enthusiasm so that people will be glad they came to the event.

You are the face that people see first. Your opening and closing enhance the overall success of the event. You are there to make people feel great for attending!

Humor is strongly encouraged if it is in good taste. This is not a stand-up comedy routine. The more formal, the less humor is necessary; but regardless, make the audience laugh at least once! Make sure you pronounce words correctly! You are the first person the audience sees and hears. You must be articulate, clear and correct!

Practice your opening comments in front of a mirror and in front of an audience of your peers. You need to see how your body moves. You want to appear controlled and in charge of the event. You need to command respect so that noise diminishes when you step onto the stage or when you stand in the front of a room.

Suggested Aids

This presentation does not require visual or audio aids. However, if you do use an aid, make sure you explain its significance before showing it. Make sure it's tasteful unless the event calls for adult references or humor.

- Pictures or video clips of people who may be in the audience are always fun and add excitement to an event

---

A SAMPLE MANUSCRIPT OUTLINE

for

The Master or Mistress of Ceremonies

(The following is a fictitious event)

INTRODUCTION

I. Are you feeling good tonight? I said, are you feeling good tonight? Do you really want to be here? Do you want to have a great time? Are you ready to rock this?
(Intrigue: rhetorical questions)

II. It is a privilege to serve as your Master/Mistress of Ceremonies for this AIDS fundraiser!
   A. We have a great cause and great people who support it!

B. Welcome to the 2008 "*We Need a Cure for AIDS . . . Now*" fundraiser! We will raise money, enjoy a good meal and have fun for the next few hours.
   (Introduce the event and your enthusiasm for being there)

III. Troy and Betty Murray started this event ten years ago when a loved one was diagnosed with this disease. They wanted to share their pain as well as their faith in believing that a cure can be discovered with more research and more love. As you know, AIDS affects everyone directly or indirectly so your presence is powerful for those who can see you tonight and for those who can not.
   (Explain the history of the event and benefits for attending)

IV. We will enjoy this delicious meal that is being served right now. We will have an unbelievable testimony by an AIDS survivor, a short slide show and finally, we will participate in the auction that will hopefully yield even more funds than we ever anticipated. It's a night of food, insight and fellowship. Thank you for being a part of the solution.
   (Preview the main points)

MEAL

Connecting words or phrases: Was that a great meal or what? Continue to finish your dessert as we embrace a young woman who contracted the AIDS virus from her husband. I wanted to properly introduce her but she insisted that I merely state: Nerosha Moy—a woman who is blessed!

BODY
   I. (Nerosha Moy's Testimony)
   (First main point with support—in this case, your first main point is someone else's presentation)

Connecting words or phrases: When I hear a testimony like that, I think to myself, "How can I possibly complain?" Let's give Nerosha another round of applause.

   II. So many live with this devastating disease that causes a lot of physical and emotional suffering. This slide presentation shows the many faces of AIDS and the strength behind those faces. Take a look.
   (Second main point—your second point is a presentation aid so you merely have to introduce the show and then mention what the audience witnessed at the end)

Connecting words or phrases: It has been an unbelievable evening. We want to conclude the event with an auction. There are several items to bid on. To conduct the auction, here is one of the city's best auctioneers . . . Mr. Bill Cux, Jr.!

CONCLUSION
   I. There was food, fellowship, and fun.
   (Indicate the end)

II. Nerosha Moy's testimony, the slide show and the auction renewed our faith in humankind . . . and human kindness.
(Summarize your main points)

III. I feel honored to have been asked to serve as your master/mistress of ceremonies. Thank you so much for coming tonight! We appreciate you! When it comes to AIDS, I'm right next to you in this battle for a cure. As Shakespeare once said, "They do not love . . . that do not *show* their love." Good night and thank you for showing YOUR love!
(Thank you and creative closures: emotional statements and a quotation)

Coel Coleman

 # THE MEETING

> *"In a good meeting there is a momentum that comes from the sponta-neous exchange of fresh ideas that produces extraordinary results. That momentum depends on the freedom permitted by the participants."*

—Harold S. Geneen (1910–97) U.S. telecommunications entrepreneur

 ## From Meaning*less* to Meaning*ful*

In the business world, meetings are inevitable. In many cases after meetings, people walk away asking, "Why did we meet again?" You have the power to take a meeting from meaningless to meaningful. The success or failure of a one-on-one meeting or a strategic planning meeting depends on *preparation, professionalism, participation,* and *pull-through.*

PREPARATION: Preparation is imperative to conduct an effective meeting.

- Create and distribute an agenda

- The meeting leader (facilitator) should prepare a clear set of goals, strategies, and points of discussion

- Consider a theme for team meetings to create excitement around the topic
  - For example, a meeting that is focused on increasing overall sales could have the theme: ***Drive Up Productivity!***

- A poorly planned meeting that is not executed correctly can lead to additional time-consuming and unproductive meetings

- Make sure all of the appropriate people will be able to attend

- The facilitator should contact all members and make sure the time and location are clear

PROFESSIONALISM

- Arrive on time (early) and show that you value the time of others
- Have set times for beginning and ending the meeting and stick to those times
- Let attendees know up front what will be discussed and what is expected of them
- Switch electronic devices to the off position
- Maintain focus and keep discussions on topic

PARTICIPATION

- Appoint a recorder-secretary to document key points and action items
- Encourage participation from all attendees. The facilitator must ensure that certain people do not monopolize the conversations
- Ensure that the group stays on topic and does not lack direction and focus
- Only one person should talk at a time
- Ideas should not be interrupted
- Be brief and concise when speaking

PULL-THROUGH

- Establish clear defined action steps
- Distribute the meeting minutes
- Distribute action charts with timelines for completion
- Follow up with correspondence (memorandums, e-mails, etc.) when tasks are completed

If you are the chairperson for a meeting, you should prepare a manuscript outline because it's still a presentation.

Elana Kornegay Thompson, M.S.
Senior Sales Professional
District Sales Trainer in the Pharmaceutical Industry
Indianapolis, IN

This section includes tips and sample manuscripts from pharmaceutical district sales trainer Elana Kornegay Thompson, M.S. and communications coordinator

Jennifer R. Coleman, M.S. Both have extensive experience with meeting planning and training others to be effective presenters.

You should have no problem with demographics for this presentation. Surveys are easy to do because you don't have to mail them and finding information about your audience is easy because there are numerous people to consult for information.

Many meetings are on-site. Some wonderful employee-centered companies or local organizations offer lunch or comfortable settings for their meetings. The on-site meeting may feel more formal and you will have to adjust your delivery and your message to reach some of the apathetic and cynical audience members who don't want to be there.

Some meetings are held off-site. Off-site meetings are more casual and workers are more receptive to news whether it's good or bad. However, there are usually more distractions when a meeting is held in a public place like a restaurant.

The time of day is crucial for setting a meeting time. Early mornings are probably best with mid-morning meetings as the close second. Meetings after lunch are very non-productive unless activity is involved and even then, most wish to take a nap. The end of the day meeting is the worst as most people will watch the clock and miss or reject most of what you have to say.

If possible, have a team or group activity! Some meetings are so routine and boring if the presenter is not an effective speaker. Use activities and demonstrations to enhance your message, even if it's a negative message. Audiences are receptive to messages that include a visual element.

Okay, it's a meeting. Do you really have to practice what you will say? YES! You still need to go over the material you will cover and the presentation aids you will use. You need to make sure your messages are in a proper order with some positive news first, the bad news in the middle and a positive claim at the end. You still need to practice and make sure you don't appear shaky and nervous with constant pacing or hand movement.

Suggested Aids

PowerPoint for staff meetings is good ONLY if pictures and minimal writing are used! There is nothing worse than being subjected to PowerPoint presentations early in the morning where the presenter reads blocks of information. BORING! Have pictures and main points with no more than four to five lines of text per slide.

Aids that would be effective at meetings:

- An object like a new coffee mug with the company logo

- An audio or video clip of an organization's television commercial

- A chart with statistics about the team's membership growth

A SAMPLE MANUSCRIPT

for

The Meeting

(ONE-ON-ONE EXISTING CLIENT)

PERSON A: Thanks for joining me today to discuss our plan to increase sales results for Quarter four. I know your time is valuable so let's get started with the items on the agenda . . . We need to discuss Q3 ideas and the budget . . . Tell me, what innovative ideas did you implement in Q3 that you would like to continue for this quarter?

PERSON B: I have reached out to increase customer relations and revenue by increasing face-to-face time with top customers. My team and I have also increased the distribution of marketing items to brand key offices.

PERSON A: What you have done has worked well. How can we achieve even greater success?

PERSON B: I would like to try to do a dinner program with a speaker in an effort to get customers to use more of our products. My team's plan is to target customers that are using more of my competitor's product. We put together these numbers and as you can see if we can win their business we would definitely meet our quarterly goals. A speaker and a banquet would be a nice way to say, "We appreciate you and we want you to make our product your number one choice."

PERSON A: That's good. This brings us to our next item on the agenda, the budget. Where do you stand with your current budget and will it accommodate a program such as this?

PERSON B: I am currently within budget. I have priced the cost of the speaker as well as the dinner cost for 200 attendees. Based on my research I will fully utilize my allocated budget and still have resources available to meet one-on one with customers.

PERSON A: Should your program exceed your budgeted amount I have additional funds that I could possibly allocate to your team. I would ask that you put together a spreadsheet of the targeted customers for attendance along with their monthly trending. We want to ensure that this dinner makes good business sense and that the appropriate customers are targeted.

PERSON B: I will get that to you Friday. I believe we have a solid plan in place and that this program would increase sales.

PERSON A: We should follow up in one week to determine if we will move forward with the program. I really like this idea and I feel confident that you and your team can make it happen.

Manuscript submitted by:
Elana Kornegay Thompson, M.S.
Senior Sales Professional
District Sales Trainer in the Pharmaceutical Industry
Indianapolis, IN

 ## Strategic Planning Meeting

Communications Coordinator Jennifer R. Coleman offers the following tips for the strategic planning meeting:

- *Adjust the meetings to fit your goals.* Depending on your goals for the strategic planning, it could take hours, days or even years of work! Many organizations strategically plan for the next 20 years!

- *Define your purpose.* Make sure you clearly define your purpose for the meeting so that the group can start to prepare for brainstorming.

- *Review the mission statement.* Make sure that you go over the mission and vision of the organization so that it is remembered during the brainstorming session.

- *Make sure that everyone in the group is engaged.* Remember to ask the group to please turn off their blackberries and cell phones so that there are no distractions during the planning sessions.

- *Do not evaluate during brainstorming.* Before brainstorming, remind the group members that there should be no evaluation of ideas until the brainstorming session is over. The purpose of brainstorming is to generate ideas, not discuss them. Discussion can take place after brainstorming, or during the next meeting.

- *Don't be afraid of silence.* It may take time for the group to loosen up and really start offering ideas. Facilitate by asking questions; but allow some silence for people to answer. If you keep talking, they are unlikely to interrupt you with their ideas.

- *Don't let the group go off topic.* During group discussions and brainstorming, it is very easy for a group to go off topic. This can happen very quickly. If you feel the meeting is going off topic, remember to bring the group members back to the main focus by reviewing the specific purpose of the meeting, while still acknowledging that the ideas are good.

- *Find a volunteer recorder/secretary.* Pick a volunteer before the meeting begins to be your "recorder/ secretary." You can use a large flip chart, marker board or even PowerPoint for your volunteer to write down the group's ideas as the brainstorming is taking place. Use whatever is the most convenient for your situation. Make sure that your audience can see what is being written. Flip charts are probably more suited for smaller groups, whereas PowerPoint on a large projector screen is better for larger groups in larger rooms.

- *Be positive and enthusiastic!* Strategic planning is a creative meeting that is meant to generate ideas. Be positive about the ideas given during brainstorming and enthusiastic about the planning process. If you look bored, your audience will be bored too!

Jennifer R. Coleman, M.S.
Communications Coordinator
Ohio Soybean Council

A SAMPLE MANUSCRIPT OUTLINE
for
The Meeting

(STRATEGIC PLANNING)

INTRODUCTION

I. A man by the name of Terence Cooke once said, "America's greatness is not only recorded in books, but it is also dependent upon each and every citizen being able to utilize public libraries."

(Intrigue: quotation)

II. As you are all aware, community involvement in the City Library has decreased significantly over the past three years. I called this meeting of the entire City Library Board of Directors because I have been an active member of this board for over 10 years now and I have seen downward trends of interest in the library.
(Introduce the topic and tell why you are qualified to speak)

III. We all serve on the library board because we all believe in the benefits a public library can offer to a community, but in order to keep it open for the next generations, we must find new ways to bring people back to the library.
(Explain the benefits of listening)

IV. While we have many challenges ahead, the main issues we need to discuss today are the decreasing use of the community meeting rooms, the decrease in books being checked out from the library and the things we could do to increase the library's popularity in the community.
(Preview the main points)

Connecting words or phrases: The upstairs meeting rooms have been an important part of this library for many years.

BODY
I. Since it was built in 1982, local businesses, government officials and schools have used the library regularly as a meeting location for a variety of activities.
  A. But according to our research, the use of the upstairs meeting rooms has decreased by 65% over the last three years! That is a big drop ladies and gentlemen.
  B. We've seen some major competition from the new hotel that was built just down the road. This hotel offers the same central location as the library, but has catering services and newly decorated meeting rooms. The hotel charges a fee for the use of its meeting rooms, and the library does not; however, the hotel's prices are not unreasonable.
  (First main point with support)

Connecting words or phrases: But the usage of the library meeting rooms is not the only library service that is struggling.

II. I think that we would all agree that checking out books is the main purpose of a library and the most significant benefit it can offer a community. The fact that this number is decreasing is a major concern.
  A. The research shows a 50% decrease in the number of books that are being checked out compared to three years ago.
  B. We believe that this decrease comes from the rising popularity of online bookstores. People seem to be more willing to pay for their books online, rather than take the time to visit the library and check them out.
  (Second main point with support)

Connecting words or phrases: Now that we've reviewed the situation, it's time to start planning for the future of the City Library.

III. While we are brainstorming, it is important to remember that the mission of the City Library is to provide free access to knowledge and to serve as a community center for educational activities. I'd like to hear your ideas for increasing the library's popularity.

A. *Brainstorming Session I* (Community Meeting Rooms)

B. *Brainstorming Session II* (Book Checkout)
   (Third main point with support)

CONCLUSION

I. It was a little difficult at times today, but this has been a great meeting.
(Indicate the end)

II. We've looked at the decreasing use of the community meeting rooms, the decrease in books being checked out from the library; and we developed ideas for what we could do to increase the library's popularity in the community.
(Summarize your main points)

III. We still have a long way to go to bring the popularity of the City Library back to what it used to be, and we'll have many more meetings like this one to accomplish that goal. But I know we all believe in the public library system and what it brings to the community. I do not intend to give up this fight, because public libraries are a part of America's greatness.
(Creative closures: emotional statements and a refer back to the intrigue)

Tips and manuscript outline submitted by:
Jennifer R. Coleman, M.S.
Communications Coordinator
Ohio Soybean Council

A SAMPLE MANUSCRIPT OUTLINE

for

The Meeting

(BASIC REPORT OF INFORMATION)

INTRODUCTION

I. So why are we here?
(Intrigue: rhetorical question)

II. Everyone has been whispering and the rumors are extensive; but today, you'll learn why we needed to change our vacation policy. I was asked to speak because I've been in the budget office for over two years now and I've seen the financial crisis this company has been going through.

(Introduce the topic and tell why you are qualified to speak)

III. This policy change affects all of us in this room but if we understand the changes we will be able to adjust our vacation dates, our family budgets and our personal time.

(Explain the benefits of listening)

IV. There are two main things that have changed: personal days have been cut from three days to two days and you will no longer be able to get your vacation money early.

(Preview the main points)

Connecting words or phrases: I know you are probably disgusted, but we can only have two personal days now.

BODY

I. Personal days have always been appreciated. I know that I have needed those days for family outings, doctor's appointments and plain old rest!

   A. Unfortunately, when people are away, we don't produce as much. This year, due to the war and other situations, we don't have as many clients. However, the work is still steady even though it hasn't been as great as previous years.

   B. With people out, it takes longer to finish our products and it puts us behind. Right now, we could not afford to take more clients if we wanted them because our man-power is too low. Therefore, we cannot afford to have too many people out at the same time and due to finances, we cannot afford to pay for more than two paid personal days. I am so very sorry but it affects me too.

(First main point with support)

Connecting words or phrases: Of course, the "good news" continues with the reason why we can't get the vacation money early.

II. In the past, all of us could get our vacation money so we could have more money when we went away. Unfortunately, we can no longer expect this to happen.

   A. Once you get your paycheck on Friday, you will not be able to get your next check until the following Friday.

      1. This is a hardship for those who looked forward to that extra money for the family trip; however, you can always go to the company Credit Union and borrow the extra money and pay it back if you need money badly.

      2. This is an option. It's not a great option; but it's an option nonetheless.

   B. The Credit Union will be very flexible with the loans since the new policies are taking effect. The loan officers will help as much as they can.

1. The Union is open Monday through Friday from 9 A.M. until 5 P.M.
2. Please use this resource if you need extra funds.
   (Second main point with support)

CONCLUSION
I. It hasn't been pleasant but at least you now know why things have changed.
   (Indicate the end)

II. So yes, it's from three days to two days and advances won't be allowed. It hurts and it affects all of us.
   (Summarize your main points)

III. But you know what? We are all here so we can earn a living for ourselves and our families and even though these are bad times, perhaps we should find something positive about this and keep our spirits alive. As someone once said, "what doesn't kill us, makes us stronger."
   (Creative closures: emotional statements and a quotation)

Coel Coleman

A SAMPLE MANUSCRIPT OUTLINE
for
The Meeting

(FOLLOW-UP REPORT)

INTRODUCTION
I. Sam Cooke sang it and now we can sing it too: "A change is going to come!"
   (Intrigue: quotation)

II. Everyone has been waiting to hear about the progress on the new parking garage. I contacted the contractor all last week and he gave me some dates and information.
   (Introduce the topic and tell why you are qualified to speak)

III. If you drive to work, this will affect you.
   (Explain the benefits of listening)

IV. There are two main areas we discussed: The date of final completion and the actual structure itself.
   (Preview the main points)

Connecting words or phrases: The estimated date for completion is May 5, 2012.

BODY

  I. This was not the original date. The construction company had lay-offs and got behind with the construction.
  - **A.** This date will allow for any delays that may occur. However, the structure may be completed well before the 2012 deadline.
  - **B.** Look for me to send quarterly updates.
    (First main point with support)

Connecting words or phrases: In addition, you may be wondering about the actual design of this garage.

  II. Actually, it is quite standard but there is one change from the original plan.
  - **A.** Originally, the entire structure was going to be covered. However, due to funding and practicality, the top floor will be uncovered.
  - **B.** Also, there will be ramps and elevators for this three-story high structure. This is necessary to accommodate all employees especially those with health challenges.
    (Second main point with support)

CONCLUSION

  I. That's all I have for now.
    (Indicate the end)

  II. Email me if you wish to know more about the date or the structure.
    (Summarize your main points)

  III. So, hang in there and stay optimistic because positive changes are definitely coming!
    (Creative closure: refer back to the intrigue)

Coel Coleman

THE NEW JOB OR PROMOTION

Even if everyone doesn't know you personally, they will be made aware of you before you speak. Be very positive since it's possible that some may not care for you personally or you may be the victim of a rumor because someone feels as if you took his or her job.

You could give remarks at the actual job site or you may be asked to give brief remarks at a public gathering where your influence is respected. Make sure your comments are brief and appropriate for the occasion. If you are only asked to say a few words, try:

It is a privilege to be the new vice-president of XYZ Company. I look forward to continue the tradition of excellence with a passion for the position and the company I represent. Thank you for your support! I look forward to serving the company and the community.

Be able to adjust to whatever setting you are in when giving these remarks. Vary the volume and expression especially if the media is involved. Remarks do require being prepared. Always be ready when you are put into a new position, to say a few words. Try to be sincere especially since someone believed in you enough to promote you or hire you. Be humble and willing to say something that shows gratitude.

Suggested Aids

None are needed but if you want to be creative:

- Pictures of yourself at your old job and at the new job
- Put on an article of clothing with your new title or company name on the front

---

A SAMPLE MANUSCRIPT OUTLINE
for
The New Job or Promotion

INTRODUCTION
   I. Someone once said, "Life is not a having and a getting but a being and becoming."
   (Intrigue: quotation)

   II. I am honored to have become the first Asian-American vice-president at this company.
   (Introduce the topic)

   III. I know ethnicity shouldn't matter but history does matter; and for those who become discouraged, perhaps this historical moment will build bridges and tear down walls.
   (Explain the benefits of listening)

   IV. I am the happiest person is this room because I believe in this company and my ability to help lead it.
   (Preview the main points)

BODY

I. I always dreamed of working for a company where the people mean just as much if not more, than the commodity it sells.

    A. I never worked for any company that gave as many days off for a job well done. It's wonderful to see you all motivated because the company believes in you.

    (First main point with support)

II. I have been here over ten years and I worked my way up from the mailroom. I loved my job as a mail clerk and I'll love my job as your vice-president.

    A. I worked hard back then and that won't change now! Hard work will test character.

    (Second main point with support)

CONCLUSION

I. I love XYZ Company and its employees that keep the quality of the products in a class by themselves.

    (Indicate the end)

II. This is a company I will always believe in and I know I have the ability to lead it.

    (Summarize your main points)

III. Thank you for your support and dedication to the vision. I'll see you in the company lounge! I'll see you because you *will* see me!

    (Creative closures: emotional statements)

Coel Coleman

THE PANEL DISCUSSION

The audience is curious about the discussion. They don't have to be there unless someone forces them to be there. If you have been asked to be a panelist, you are

considered qualified to be an expert on a topic. A panel discussion can take place at any time during the day. It's usually no more than an hour. The first few minutes will be spent introducing the panelists and the topic. At least twenty or thirty minutes will be used for open discussion and then the last part of the time allotted will be for audience questions. If you are the panelist or the moderator, have a glass of water with you.

You don't have to rehearse anything! You just need to think on your feet and be well-versed and knowledgeable about the topic. You could have a friend ask you some questions to make sure you are ready for the forum that includes audience questions. Public forums usually follow panel discussions or team symposiums so you want to be controlled and poised when you answer questions especially if some of the audience members are hostile.

Suggested Aids

If aids are used, they are usually not used by the panelists. The moderator may show a dramatic video clip to evoke emotion or a graph with statistical data. However, the panelists and their opinions are the main focus for a panel discussion.

A SAMPLE MANUSCRIPT
for
The Panel Discussion

(The following names and dialogue are fictitious)

INTRODUCTION (by the moderator)
How can so many students who make outstanding academic grades, wind up making such bad personal decisions?
(Intrigue: question)

Welcome to this afternoon's discussion entitled: "The numbers are up because the ability to say 'no' is down—A look at the rise in teenage drinking and alcohol-related deaths." I'm Mulan Parks your moderator.
(Introduction of the topic and the moderator)

During the next forty-five minutes, we will explore this serious topic that is still prevalent in our nation despite the programs, the lectures and the statistics. Young people are still engaging in underage drinking and then driving under the influence thus putting you and your loved ones at risk.
(Explain the benefits of listening)

We have three panelists who are experts with this subject. Our first panelist is local police chief Ike Stevie who has seen more teens drink and drive than he wants to admit. He'll give some statistics and cite some experiences he has encountered at his job. Our respondents are Carla Masters and Paula Pauling. Carla Masters is the chairperson of People Against Drunk Teens Driving. Her daughter died when her friend drove drunk after a high school graduation party. She has spoken around the country and she's an advocate for strict penalties for drunk drivers. We also have Paula Pauling who is a seventeen year-old high school student who is now paralyzed because she hit a tree while drinking and driving.

(Introduction of the panelists)

MODERATOR: Let's start with a basic question. The underage drinking is bad enough but why are these teens still driving? Chief . . . what's going on?

BODY

STEVIE: It is alarming. These kids are trying to fit in so they give in to peer pressure. I guess I can get the peer pressure but I just don't get the drunk driving. Underage drinking has never really changed that much over the years. But we in law enforcement had hoped our visits to schools and our videos with graphic scenes would curb their driving under the influence. Now, in some instances, it has worked; but unfortunately, there are still too many who drink and don't have designated drivers. This year, I have told over 30 sets of parents that their children were never coming back home. For me, it's horrible. I have children and I can only imagine having someone tell me that . . . especially over something so careless!

MODERATOR: We know you and your staff have been to the schools. When no one is watching, what are the underage drinkers saying about why they take risks even when they know they could kill themselves or others?

STEVIE: They don't have an answer and that's the crazy part. They really don't have an answer. I actually asked a group of students a few months ago and they all stared at me a few seconds before one brave young girl finally spoke up and said, "We never think it will happen to us . . . we know drinking and driving is dangerous and stupid; but when drunk, people think they can handle anything." That was a scary interview. The kids said they just wanted to be a part of the crowd and the people they went to parties with all wanted to drink so it was hard to get a designated driver who wasn't a drinker too.

MASTERS: I know. My daughter died at a party where she was also drinking. I didn't want to believe it because she was such a great student. She was the stereotype of the All-American girl. She was pretty, and smart and popular. She had a boyfriend who was handsome and smart and popular. It just makes me sick now because when I hear a parent speak of how perfect his or her child is, I just want to scream: DO YOU REALLY KNOW WHAT YOUR KID IS DOING WHEN YOU'RE NOT WATCHING! My daughter and her friend were both intoxicated when they got into that car. I was furious at Shelby for years. I kept asking her why she drove drunk and why they didn't call me or someone to drive them home. But after awhile, I realized how stupid I was for blaming her. Shelby did what so many do. They deny they are impaired. They have beer goggles on that say everything looks wonderful. That's what alcohol does. It's not like I wasn't a teenager. I wasn't perfect. As horrified as I still am, I know it wasn't just Shelby's fault. My daughter Pamela had a choice to not get in that car. She made her choice. Her choice took her life.

MODERATOR: I see hands. I'll take a question after we let Miss Pauling say a few words.

PAULING: I know what Mrs. Masters is saying. I'm paralyzed and I personally never drank a day in my life. But I can't be bitter because although I don't drink, I have done other rebellious things. Actually, I'm a lot closer to my family now because I share things I never would have shared. I want them to know I'm not perfect either and that a drunk driver hurt me but I won't condemn him for that. I asked to meet him when I was in the hospital. He didn't want to face me. His mom said he wanted to pretend it never happened. He was in college at the time and he wanted to suppress the night it happened. But I wanted to see him. I forgave him but he needed to see the reality of his actions while also knowing that his victim forgave him. He finally came to visit and it was powerful for both of us. He and I still chat on the internet at least once a week. He's also married now and doing well. He has given to a charity in my name which isn't necessary; but I guess he feels better giving something back. I told him the best thing he could do was to not drink and drive ever again. I told him that when he has kids, to make sure he is aware of what they are doing at all times ... as much as possible. Sometimes there are signs.

MODERATOR: What kind of signs?

PAULING: Well, not major signs ... just pay attention to how much they go out ... or if they don't go out at all but finally get asked to a party. I'd be careful of that ...

MODERATOR: Okay, we'll take a few questions ... gentleman in the back with the blue polo ... what is your question and who is it for?

QUESTION: I'm a father who believes he knows his son but now I'm worried. I can't be with him all day!

MODERATOR: What is the question and who is it for?

QUESTION: My question is, if I ask too many questions won't my son be more inclined to rebel? I guess I'm asking the young girl.

PAULING: I know what you're asking. Kids will do what they want to do regardless but we are more inclined to call home or even tell parents something if the lines of communication seem to be open. You don't have to encourage drinking but keep assuring your son that he can come to you about anything and you will give YOUR opinion without downing his opinion. Then, when he asks serious questions and sees that you validate his opinions, even if you disagree, he will probably discuss the parties and stuff with you because he feels he won't be yelled at.

QUESTION: Can I just follow-up? It will be really short.

MODERATOR: Not at this time ... we need to move on ... let me take a question from the lady in the red shirt ... in the back.

QUESTION: My question is for Chief Stevie. Will the police pick up my daughter from a party if she calls drunk and asks for help? Would you really have time to do that?

STEVIE: The police will patch into the local cab company that we deal with. We cannot personally come out unless some impending crime is happening because our force is so understaffed and the demand in the city is so great. However, we have recently linked up with "Cabs For U" and they will get your child home safely. However, information will be taken and we will record it. If this person is constantly calling, the parents will be notified and the service for this person may be terminated. However, we are aware of safety so it's unlikely we would let a drunk person drive home.

MODERATOR: Mrs. Masters, do you wish to add something?

MASTERS: Yes. People Against Drunk Teens Driving also has a cab service. I have cards that I will leave on the table out front. PLEASE pick some up and distribute them to your children, their friends and put them wherever you can. We must stop drunk drivers. We will pick up anyone who calls. We ask them to pay a fee but if they don't have money and they are visibly intoxicated, we will still take them home. We don't want them driving. We are primarily funded by donations. All of our information is on the card. Please take some and pass them out.

MODERATOR: Time is running out so let's have each panelist give some final comments.

(SUMMATIONS)

CONCLUSION (by the moderator)

I. We can't reach a solution tonight but we certainly have opened our ears and minds to alternate ways of thinking about this problem that affects all us directly or indirectly. **(Indicate the end)**

II. We thank Chief Stevie, Mrs. Masters and Miss Pauling for sharing their insight about this problem that affects all of us. Again, the statistics mentioned are all on the police department and PADTD websites. We are out of time but I'm sure the panelists are willing to answer some more questions if you catch them before they leave! **(Thank all of the panelists)**

III. Thank you for being a part of this discussion. Never say, "My child wouldn't drink and drive." Be realistic. Be informed. Be aware of what your children are really doing when you're not watching. Be smart. **(Creative closures: emotional statements)**

Coel Coleman

People want to be inspired and motivated to be the best they can be. From the commencement to the annual conference, people have been waiting all year for that special speech from that special person. You are that person! You were asked to be the main event so you have to bring it! It doesn't matter what the demographics are. The attitudes and values will vary. Your job is to make people feel empowered and moved to change and improve themselves and others.

Image © JupiterImages Corp., 2009.

A keynote is usually an after-dinner speech. It may be right after a meal and part of a banquet. It could be late in the morning and right before lunch. It could be at any time BUT it is rare for a keynote address to be before 10 A.M. It's usually around lunch or dinner/supper or as a late night opening ceremony speech for a weekend conference.

Microphones are a must! Wear a lavaliere microphone even if you have a podium/lectern because this way you can walk around. A keynote should involve some animated movement so that emotional levels are high. Make sure you are loud, articulate and expressive. Your presentation outline should be typed and placed into a conservative portfolio that compliments your attire; but you can never go wrong with basic black. Memorize the introduction and conclusion. Know your presentation well enough to lose your place and yet know where you are in your presentation.

Suggested Aids

- PowerPoint slides of pictures or data can be effective but MINIMAL use is encouraged.

- Handouts are not great if the audience is large. Paper can be noisy so any information that can be put on a slide or the use of a large object would be best

Let your words and the way you say them be the focus of a keynote address. Vivid language and a strong delivery will surpass the effectiveness of aids any day. Most famous speakers are remembered for speeches that had few if any presentation aids.

President Obama is giving a persuasive keynote address.

A SAMPLE MANUSCRIPT OUTLINE

for

The Persuasive Keynote Address

(For people who embrace positive changes)

INTRODUCTION

I. We have problems . . . in our country . . . in our homes . . . in our souls.
    (Intrigue: emotional statements)

II. We have problems in our country when our children know more about condoms than financial planning. We have problems in our homes when we care more about how our children look to others rather than how they *really* feel about themselves. We have problems in our souls when we preach the things we never practice because it's easier to point fingers outward rather than point fingers inward. We have problems; but I'm not talking to anyone in this room, right?

    I'm talking about those *other* people.

    Now, of course, who am I to even say these things? I'm just a stranger. You know, the director of youth services at some organization that works with local kids who have nowhere to go after school . . . I'm just the stranger who they asked to come speak to you today because they needed a speaker.
    (Introduce the subject and tell why you are qualified to speak)

III. The things I say are not things that really apply to you personally . . . right? So, just ignore whatever isn't applicable to you. I certainly wouldn't want to offend anyone . . . actually make anyone look deep inside to see if he or she is part of the problem . . . I wouldn't do that. Why would self-reflection change the country, the home, the soul?

(Explain the benefits of listening)

IV. So for those *other* people . . . help me to let them know that they should get honest and get active.

(Preview the main points)

Connecting words or phrases: Tell those other people to get honest.

BODY

I. Honesty is the first step towards changing the outside or the inside.

    A. People say they are honest and yet I see beautiful cars driven by sad faces.

        1. I recently conducted a survey at a local mall . . . in an area of the city that is perceived to be affluent.

        2. One in four adults said they were content but not really happy.

        3. They said that they wished their families were more strong and loving.

    B. People say they are honest and yet I see gifts wrapped in beautiful tissue paper and opened by those who drink to dull the pain.

        1. They smoke to ease the nervousness associated with being overworked and underpaid.

        2. Or they take pills to sleep because depression tells them the gifts they can afford to give, are not good enough and they feel ashamed.

    C. Those *other people* say they are honest and yet I also see designer logos on purses, luggage and shirts owned by people who cry "why don't they really love me and have time for me?"

(First main point with support)

Connecting words or phrases: Getting honest means you know that at some point you have been one of the *other* people . . . even if you did your best to never act like *them*.

II. With honesty, people have the desire to change . . . to get active.

    A. It doesn't take more money or more effort, to spend more time with your family. It only takes more love and more insight. Turn off the gadgets and put down the paper and talk to your children. That's all they want and that's *most* of what they need.

    B. Gerald was a well-intentioned father. He worked ten hour shifts each day to provide for his three children and for his wife. When his oldest daughter started acting funny, Gerald ignored the signs. He ignored her quiet demeanor. He ignored her change in clothing styles. He ignored her new friends. He was busy. He was tired. He was making money. It wasn't until after she got shot, that the bullet pierced his soul and made him wake up to realize that all of his efforts were in his providing the physiological needs while ignoring his daughter's self-actualization needs.

C. He had forgotten how to be a father in the most basic sense. He forgot how to hug his family when he came home. He forgot how to mandate family dinners instead of allowing his kids to eat whenever and with whomever. But once his daughter was almost killed, he changed. He got active in the lives of all of his children . . . and it did not take more money . . . it took more love.

(Second main point with support)

CONCLUSION

I. Why is this the keynote address for XYZ Corporation? Why am I not talking about products or numbers or employee rights? It's simple . . . because what you bring to work with you—will ultimately determine what happens *to* you.

(Indicate the end)

II. Get honest so that you have the desire and energy to get active. Take care of your country by minimizing your potential to be one of the *other* people. Take care of your homes so that when you come to work you feel energized and not victimized. Take care of your soul . . . don't sell that. Take care of your soul with your mind focused on important things and not on superficial things.

(Summarize your main points)

III. With honesty and energy, we can make changes that affect all of us and those we work with. We have problems in our country . . . in our homes . . . and in our souls . . . but with honesty and action, those problems can just be hurdles for all of us to jump over on our way to the finish line, where we embrace our gold medals. Where we embrace our team victory. Let's change us . . . and let's change now! Get honest. Get active. Get ready!

(Creative closures: emotional statements)

Coel Coleman

 ## THE PRESENTATION OF AN AWARD OR GIFT

(*Also see* The Acceptance of an Award or Gift)

You have the pleasure of presenting an honor to someone who deserves it. You need to be genuine, well-rehearsed, poised and enthusiastic! If you have a bland performance, you will dishonor the recipient. Just like introducing a speaker, it's your job to build excitement for this individual and for the audience.

Make sure you either know the recipient, have the opportunity to speak to the recipient, or have the chance to check all the information you are about to say about the recipient. You need to make sure you have his or her name correct. Make sure the accomplishments you are about to state, are correct. Make sure the information is tasteful and complete. Practice this presentation.

Corporate Development Specialist and Professor of Communication Karen Hill Johnson shares her example of a speech of presentation. (See her example of The Acceptance of an Award or Gift)

Suggested Aids

This very short speech does not need an aid other than the object you are presenting.

A SAMPLE MANUSCRIPT OUTLINE
for
The Presentation of an Award or Gift

INTRODUCTION

  I. "I call it like I see it," "On your feet," "Just keeping it real."
    (Intrigue: quotations)

  II. These quotes are just a few we hear from this professor in the Speech Communication Department at West Eastern University.
    (Introduce the topic)

  III. The students have voted and this year, the vote was unanimous. I am proud to say I was one of the students who voted for this wonderful professor who touched my life two years ago when I was in her class.
    (Tell why you are qualified to speak)

  IV. Today, you will know the reasons why students chose this educator for the distinguished "Profound Professor Award" before I tell you about the recipient.
    (Preview the main points)

Connecting words or phrases: First, let's hear the reasons why the students voted for this profound professor.

BODY

  I. When submitting nominations for this award, students supported their votes with the following comments:
    A. "This professor actually made me work for my A."

B. "She called me out when I was slacking and because of that, I really applied myself for the first time as a student."

C. "She set me up for success with encouraging words and realistic objectives."

D. "Through tough-love, she showed me how to be the best I could be."

(First main point with support)

Connecting words or phrases: Now that we know why the students voted for this professor, let's find out more about who she is.

II. This professor can be seen in her office outside of scheduled office hours coaching students on their persuasive speeches, buying stock-piles of red ink pens for grading, driving the 15-passanger van to speech competitions.

A. She motivates students through her honest dialogue and pushes us to reach our ultimate potential.

B. This professor goes above and beyond to influence students in a positive way even if we hate it at first! She calls us. She emails us. She shows up at our houses when we pretend to be sick. It's intimidating but also refreshing.

(Second main point with support)

CONCLUSION

I. There's so much I could say but I promised I would be brief.
(Indicate the end)

II. There are so many reasons she is deserving of this honor and I am proud to be the one to present it to such a worthy person.
(Summarize your main points)

III. Because this professor goes above and beyond the standard of excellence through her dedication and sincere concern for students, the 2008 Profound Professor Award goes to Dr. Chris Wilson Hall
(Creative closure: emotional statement)

Manuscript outline submitted by:
Karen Hill Johnson, M.S.
Corporate Development Specialist
Professor of Communication
Mid-Continent University

 # THE PRESS CONFERENCE

There are usually two audiences for a press conference. The first audience is physically with the speakers. This audience is comprised of some local dignitaries, media professionals, government officials and citizens. The second audience is made up of television viewers. The press conference is probably in a large room with decent acoustics. Many people will stand up so they can take pictures or get the best position to ask questions during the forum.

Image © U.P.images_vector, 2009. Used under license from Shutterstock, Inc.

Practice is preferred but some press conferences are extremely impromptu. Be well-spoken and prepared or let someone else more experienced handle the press. Although a prepared manuscript is not required, you need to know the information. You do not want to seem dazed and confused. Your behavior will calm the public or incite a panic. Be calm and correct!

Your language needs to be concrete and not ambiguous. Your verbal quality should be articulate, loud enough and full of vocal variety. In the following sample manuscript, David A. Yastremski, M.S. offers this example of a press conference. Mr. Yastremski has years of communication expertise in the public school system, university setting and corporate environment. (See his example for The Debate.)

Suggested Aids

Presentation aids are not usually used but in some circumstances, they can really help clarify the situation:

- A satellite shot of the impending storm

- A large picture of damage to the building or the vehicles

- A German shepherd sitting next to you, that will be the lead dog in the search for the missing child

---

A SAMPLE MANUSCRIPT
for
The Press Conference

(The following names and dialogue are fictitious)

TIPS: Greet the media beforehand with clear instructions on where to set up cameras, microphones, and lighting. In some cases, a press packet should be distributed with pertinent and necessary details about the state of the situation.

MODERATOR: Good morning and thank you for attending. We would like to brief you on the current situation as of 8:00 A.M., regarding the power outage as result of last night's weather. Speaking today will be Jane Smith (S-M-I-T-H), the mayor of Anytown, John Dwyer (D-W-Y-E-R), the director of Anytown Power and Light, and Captain Adam Evans (E-V-A-N-S), Sheriff of Anytown . . . Okay, Mayor Smith if you would start us off with a report.

MAYOR SMITH: Good morning, because of a line of thunderstorms that went through Anytown between the hours of 9:00 P.M. and 10:00 P.M. last night, a portion of the city has been without power for the past ten hours. At 11:00 P.M., 750 homes were reported without power and overnight, crews worked to begin restoration. Currently, approximately 400 homes are still without power, along with several non-essential municipal services. Anytown Power and Light has been working around the clock to have power restored as quickly as possible to avoid any other inconvenience to the families and businesses. The Anytown Police Department and Social Services have maintained an active presence in the affected areas, offering services to citizens and directing them to the necessary resources. We thank everybody for their patience and ask full cooperation by everyone to help maintain a safe and secure environment while we work diligently to rectify the situation.

MODERATOR: Thank you. We now will hear from Mr. Dwyer, the director of Anytown Power and Light.

MR. DWYER: Thank you. At 9:34 P.M., last night, lightning struck a transformer, causing power failure for the majority of western Anytown. In addition, several downed power lines, because of wind and debris, were reported in the southwestern portion of the municipality. Crews are currently working overtime to restore power as quickly as possible. We hope to have all power restored by 6:00 P.M. this evening. In the meantime, we want to ask residents with power to limit their consumption to essential use only. In addition, if anyone discovers any downed power lines, please stay away from them and notify the police immediately. It should also be noted that APL power and cooling stations have been set up for families and pets at the following locations: Kennedy High School on Main Street and Anytown Community College on College Boulevard. Anyone who needs power or relief from the heat will find food, shelter, and power, including refrigeration for medication and other purposes, at those two locations.

MODERATOR: Next, we will hear from Sheriff Evans.

SHERIFF EVANS: Police crews have been monitoring the streets and affected areas around the clock to help direct traffic. They are offering assistance when needed. We have increased troop patrols near the business district on Main Street. Thanks to the cooperation of everyone, there have been only a few incidents. We ask the cooperation of the entire town as municipal service employees work to restore power. We also ask that 911 be reserved for emergencies only; if you have a question regarding any non-emergency issue, please call the Anytown hotline at 311. Again, please leave 911 for emergency use only. The city of Anytown is committed to their emergency response system and we are responding to all calls as quickly as we can. Again, if anyone discovers downed wires or large debris of any kind, they are encouraged to call 911 immediately so we can investigate the situation. Under no circumstances should anyone go near any downed wires or attempt to move any large debris. Police and social service personnel are also stationed at the power and cooling centers at the high school and at the community college.

MODERATOR: We will now entertain questions.

REPORTER 1: Sheriff, have any incidents been reported regarding looting or theft?

SHERIFF EVANS: No, the only specific police responses have been related to traffic moving violations.

REPORTER 1: How many?

SHERIFF EVANS: Since the power outage at 9:35 P.M., there have been eleven traffic citations.

REPORTER 1: Were these the result of the power outage?

SHERIFF EVANS: I cannot comment on the cause of those incidents.

REPORTER 2: Sheriff, has the hospital or other emergency services been affected by the power outage?

SHERIFF EVANS: The hospital's emergency generators supplied power until we were able to restore full power to the hospital at approximately 12:30 P.M. this morning. The police station and other emergency services were not affected by the power outage.

REPORTER 3: Mayor, has any emergency crisis plan been enacted by the town?

MAYOR SMITH: No, this has not been categorized as an emergency situation at this time. The public and safety personnel have been working hard to help restore power and to provide services without disruption. We are confident that power will be restored by early evening, so that all Anytown businesses and services will be up and running tomorrow.

REPORTER 4: Mayor, have there been any accommodations for the disabled or elderly who might have a hard time getting to the power and cooling stations?

MAYOR SMITH: We have several shuttles making pickups for those individuals and families who may need help. If anyone needs assistance in reaching the high school or community college, he/she can call 311 to make arrangements.

REPORTER 5: How long will the stations remain open and is there food and water available?

MAYOR: The stations will remain open until the appropriate time when power has been restored. Area businesses have been providing food, water, and other essentials for any displaced individuals and families.

REPORTER 5: Mr. Dwyer, there has been a rumor of some misappropriation of funds in Anytown Power and Light, do you have a comment?

Mr. Dwyer: Our current priority is re-instating power to our customers. I will not comment on anything else at this time.

Reporter 5: Sheriff, do you have enough manpower to sustain this crisis?

Sheriff Evans: Yes, we have plenty of public and safety personnel who are working diligently to preserve order, safety, and security in Anytown. The citizens should know that we will continue to do so until everything is back in order.

Reporter 5: Mr. Dwyer, what is the likelihood that full power will be restored by 6:00 P.M. this evening?

Mr. Dwyer: At this time, we're fully confident and making every attempt to have all power restored to our customers by that time. If anything should arise that will not allow us to accomplish this, we will let the sheriff's office and media know immediately so everyone can make the necessary preparations and plans.

Moderator: We will be providing updates as the situation progresses. I want to thank everyone for their assistance and cooperation as we work to resolve this situation. I want to remind everyone to use the 311 hotline with any questions or concerns regarding the power situation. All emergency requests should call into 911. We hope to have another update later today. Up-to-date information will continue to be available on the municipality's website. Thank you very much. Let's continue to work together to recover from this incident!

Tips and manuscript submitted by:
David A. Yastremski, M.S.
Educator and Consultant
Bernards Township Public Schools
Basking Ridge, New Jersey

THE PROPOSAL

Most likely, someone from the audience has invited you to make a proposal. Therefore, the audience members want to hear what you have to say. The members need to be those who can actually make a decision about your proposal. Therefore, you have to present when it's convenient for them since you want your proposal accepted. Be prepared for any type of seating but ask in advance about the location, technology and seating options.

Always practice a proposal presentation. It's definitely a prepared speech. Be ready for questions at any point during the presentation and be prepared to fall right back into where you left off. Practice with any technology that you want to use especially if you have never used the equipment before! You don't want to have any technical difficulty or your credibility will be affected. Go to the actual location if that is possible.

Suggested Aids

- PowerPoint slides with bullets for each subject area you discuss

- A typed handout of the actual proposal but make sure that people turn the pages when you instruct them to turn so they can focus on your presentation and not on your aid.

A SAMPLE MANUSCRIPT OUTLINE

for

The Proposal

INTRODUCTION

I. If your students can be the best, why settle for just okay?
(Intrigue: question)

II. This Student Development Office has perceived a need for advanced training in the area of student leadership. It's my understanding that you want a seminar that will help to improve communication skills and strengthen relationships between the student leaders and the teams they supervise. My proposed workshop is designed to help participants develop effective interpersonal, small group/team communication and conflict management skills.
(Introduce the topic)

III. I'm a recent graduate of this university and my degree and experience involve leadership training. As you saw from my resume, I have conducted over ten workshops and I have participated in several seminars and conferences. I was happy when the office asked me to prepare a proposal to train current and future undergraduate leaders at this university.
(Tell why you are qualified to speak)

IV. First, I will explain the benefits of this seminar and the course of instruction; secondly, I'll share the details involved like time and materials; and finally, I'll reveal the cost for this outstanding opportunity to improve productivity and student morale within organizations.
(Preview the main points)

Connecting words or phrases: What are the benefits; what is involved; and how will I conduct this seminar?

BODY

  I. It is believed that the current student mentor-mentee relationships could be improved significantly by utilizing team communication principles and leadership strategies.

    A. Although, a scientific study has not been conducted for the purpose of this proposal, it is reasonable to assume that students excel more when they are in an atmosphere that promotes that student and his or her goals.

        1. The acquisition of interpersonal, team communication and conflict management skills results from an activity-oriented training program where participants apply theory through role-playing.

        2. There will also be some case discussion and feedback. I will introduce the theories and conduct small group activities which purposely produce strong emotions.

        3. There will be in depth analysis and problem-solving discussions. With this approach as an instructor, I am a learning facilitator rather than a lecturer.

    B. The core content of the seminar/workshop will include team and trust building, listening, nonverbal communication, deviant personality behaviors and how to handle them, gender and culture awareness, types of leaders, leadership strategies, problem solving and decision-making group techniques, conflict resolution, group roles, planning business meetings, and distributing the agenda. **(PowerPoint slide)**

(First main point with support: benefits and course of instruction)

Connecting words or phrases: Now, what materials are needed and what time frame are we talking about?

  II. I will primarily utilize information from the text *Team Communication For All* by Irma and Delores. (fictitious citation)

    A. The participants will be given handouts and case studies for role-playing and for discussions.

        1. A television with a DVD or a computer will be needed so that movie clips can be shown.

    B. Unless the university finds a need to extend it, this seminar will consist of two three hour sessions over a one day period.

        1. I will train from 8:00 A.M.–11 A.M. and from 12:30 P.M.–3:30 P.M.

        2. There will be an hour and a half lunch break.

        (Second main point with support: materials and time)

Connecting words or phrases: You know everything except the number of people I can accommodate and the cost.

  III. The number of full day participants could range from 12 to 50 depending on the space you provide.

A. It is advisable that if more than 50 people need training, then separate workshops could be conducted on separate days.

    I. However, flexibility is a must; and despite any possible constraints, any student leader can participate.

B. All teaching and learning materials will be provided by me.

    I. Based on a one day, six hour seminar, I will design, prepare and deliver a program for $2495.00 plus travel and copy expenses.

    (Third main point with support: participants and cost)

CONCLUSION

  I. I think it's wonderful that a university thinks that "just okay" isn't good enough.
(Indicate the end)

  II. My proposal that includes the benefits, the content, the materials, the cost, etc. can be implemented right away.
(Summarize your main points)

  III. I have experience. I have great ideas. I have a proposal. You have a choice so make the right one. Because as Jean Nidetch once said, "It's choice—not chance that determines your destiny."
(Creative closures: emotional statements and a quotation)

Coel Coleman

THE RELIGIOUS SERVICE

Regardless of your denomination, spiritual practices or religious philosophies, presentations for a religious occasion require preparation and evidence in accordance to the area being highlighted. If your faith or lack thereof has a primary source, then that source should be quoted throughout the presentation. Make sure the source is regarded as one of authority or your message may not be well-received.

The audience will also expect you to be clear, articulate, trustworthy and well-informed. Pastor Darrell R. Young of Calvary Temple in Murray, Kentucky has over 35 years in the ministry. He shares his message in the sample manuscript outline. He and his wife Shad enjoy sharing the Word of God. Regardless of your beliefs, be organized and in all your getting—get understanding.

Pastor Darrell R. Young delivers a mid-week religious message.

Suggested Aids

- Show a book like the Holy Bible or any written material that supports your message

- Use objects like bowls, blankets, etc. when you have demonstrations of principles

- Have people dress in clothing that reflect the people in the lesson

- Show multi-media clips or pictures of dramatic images to create strong emotions from the listeners since most presentations are persuasive in nature

---

A SAMPLE MANUSCRIPT OUTLINE

for

The Religious Service

(Sermon entitled "Seed of Faith")

NEW KING JAMES VERSION OF THE HOLY BIBLE

Text: Luke 17:5, 6—*"And the apostles said to the Lord, 'Increase our faith.' So the Lord said, 'If you have faith as a mustard seed, you can say to this mulberry tree, be pulled up by the roots and be planted in the sea, and it would obey you.'"*

INTRODUCTION

I. A mustard seed is very small in size compared to other seeds such as a walnut or an acorn. Here's a walnut. Here's a mustard seed.
    (Intrigue: emotional action with presentation aids)

II. A seed is a symbol of faith. The apostles were concerned about the size of their faith. Jesus explained that it was not the size of their faith which helped them to achieve their goals.
    (Introduce the topic)

III. Environmental elements are the key to growth, like a healthy atmosphere and a strong inner faith.
    (Preview the main points)

Connecting words or phrases: Our environments are so important!

BODY

I. A good seed of any kind will not produce the right results as long as it remains in an unsuitable atmosphere.
    A. An individual who is seeking truth, direction for his or her life, setting goals, or trying to get through a crisis, has a good seed within.

B. Everyone has a measure of faith-a seed within. But for it to be nurtured, it needs to be planted in good soil-in a good environment.

C. For example, the late George Muller felt convinced that God had called him to a life-long mission to provide orphanages for children. This was his mission of faith. However, there was a twist to his mission. It was to be debt-free and no advertising was to be used. Muller refused association with those who were well-intended, well-known, but doubtful of his mission. He surrounded himself with like-minded people who shared the same faith. And for more than sixty years, thousands of children were provided for.

(First main point with support)

Connecting words or phrases: The atmosphere must be healthy and then your inner faith must be strengthened.

II. The right environment for a seed to grow and produce involves adequate water, oxygen, temperature and light. These are a must. (Germination)

A. For the seed of faith to produce, a believer should be in the right atmosphere surrounded by a strong belief in God as we know Him, positive influences, discipline, and knowledge about setting goals and reaching them.

B. Romans 10:8 states, *"The Word is near you, even in your mouth and in your ear."* That is the word of faith which we preach. All of us have goals, challenges, and desires. We all have questions that need to be answered. That is why faith is so important.

C. Charles Spurgeon once said "Faith is hard because it is easy. It is difficult because there is no difficulty in it. And it seems obscure simply because it is so clear."

CONCLUSION

I. Are you seeking answers? Is there a goal you would like to achieve? Or are you going through a crisis?

(Indicate the end)

II. Let your environment be surrounded by the key elements . . . a healthy atmosphere and inner faith builders. Surround yourselves with the right people, the right resources, the right spiritual guidance. Faith may be small like a seed, but if planted in the right environment it will produce powerful results.

(Summarize your main points)

III. Our entire lives are based on faith. Faith is a God-given gift that we have in order to find fulfillment and purpose. And the first step in the right direction is finding . . . Him.

(Creative closures: emotional statements)

Manuscript outline submitted by:
Darrell R. Young
Pastor
Calvary Temple
Murray, Kentucky

THE REPORT OF RESEARCH FINDINGS

The audience is usually not hostile. Many members will have formal educations and they will be accustomed to case studies, journal article reviews or basic research findings. There will probably be a classroom seating arrangement with you at the front and everyone else seated in rows. The focus will be on your information and analysis.

In a written report you would need a cover page, letter of transmittal, table of contents, list of figures and tables, an abstract, etc. However, an oral presentation for research findings (answering a basic research question or reviewing a journal article or case study) requires the standard manuscript outline with an introduction and a body that might include a summary of the findings, theory analysis, methods and procedures, and the results of your study. The conclusion will have your research conclusions and necessary recommendations before closing with a creative closure.

Answering a research question involves theory analysis and a review of the literature. Make sure your analysis is sound and the question that was asked is actually answered during your presentation. The case study and article reviews are similar but not identical. If you have to review an article, make sure you summarize the article first, tell a little about the author who wrote the article, and then give your educated opinion

based on personal knowledge and research. Author information must be correct and current or preface your comments by letting the audience know that the information is not current. However, your credibility as a presenter could be affected. Make sure you cite any and all research that you conduct as you present your opinions.

The following is an example of a report for answering a research question. Graduate student April René Payne shares a portion of her presentation for her senior capstone course. April was the president of her college Speech and Debate Union and a four-year multiple award winner for public address and argumentation.

Suggested Aids

- PowerPoint slides showing data are fine but not necessary. YOU should be the primary presentation aid.

- A typed handout of the case study or data would be appropriate. Make sure all handouts have some color.

A SAMPLE MANUSCRIPT OUTLINE

for

The Report of Research Findings

(Answering a Basic Research Question)

HOW DO PERSUASIVE COMMUNICATION AND ORGANIZATIONAL POLITICS AFFECT DECISION-MAKING BY CONGRESS?

INTRODUCTION

I. Abraham Zaleznick once said, "Whatever else organizations may be . . . they are political structures. This means that organizations operate by distributing authority and setting a stage for the exercise of power."

(Intrigue: quotation)

II. The context of Congress was explored as I conducted my research in my field of organizational communication. It is said that the United States government is "by the people, for the people." Yet, this organization's decisions are those we must abide by, whether we want to or not. Congress is not a religious organization where we can choose to tolerate the rules of a particular faith if we want to. It is not a non-profit organization that we can choose to donate our money or time to, if we want to. Congress is an organization with laws and regulations we are forced to obey or face the consequences. And that is what makes it so different.

(Introduce the topic and tell why you are qualified to speak)

III. By learning how persuasive communication and organizational politics affect the decisions that are made by Congress, we are analyzing and learning something that is pertinent to all of us.

(Explain the benefits of listening)

IV. Today, we will answer the question "How do persuasive communication and organizational politics affect decision-making by Congress" by examining the definition and variables of persuasive communication and organizational politics before answering the question.

(Preview the main points)

Connecting words or phrases: First, we have to define persuasive communication.

BODY

I. Persuasive communication is a form of communication that every human has engaged in.

    A. For some, it comes naturally. For others, it takes experience and understanding to perfect.

        1. According to K.E. Anderson author of *Persuasion, Theory and Practice,* the process itself is defined as "The conscious attempt to modify thought and action by manipulating the motives of men toward pre-determined ends."

    B. According to Conrad and Poole in their text *Strategic Organizational Communication* (2005) there are three categories of persuasion: open persuasion, manipulative persuasion and manipulation.

        1. Open persuasion is when the motive is clear for the target audience. Tactics such as bargaining and cooperation are often utilized.

        2. Manipulative Persuasion occurs "when the influencer disguises his or her strategy, but not the goal." An example of this would be "going over" someone's head to get what you want. The individuals involved do not see you as manipulative per se, but you are being manipulative by disguising how you are getting to the goal.

        3. The final persuasive category is Manipulation. This occurs when one disguises both the goal and strategy. Alarmingly, this is the most common organizational strategy. Understanding and recognizing the different categories of persuasive strategies has incredible implications for organizations.

        (First main point with support)

Connecting words or phrases: Now that we understand persuasive communication, let us examine the second variable of organizational politics.

II. Politics.

    A. The very word can send people into a state of euphoria discussing campaigns, elections, and members of their own or opposing political parties.

        1. Others hear the word and it brings about a sense of uncertainty or indifference. However, politics invariably exist in every organization, including Congress.

        2. According to the article *Power and Politics* from the Texas Tech website Division of Outreach and Extended Studies accessed yesterday, organizational politics can be defined as: "Those activities taken within organizations to acquire, develop, and use power and other resources to obtain one's preferred outcome …"

    B. Research explains that if the status quo increases, then there is an increase in organizational politics.

        1. Why is this? Because most individuals do not like change. Therefore, in order to maintain the status quo, we do whatever it takes … even engaging in organizational politics to make sure things stay the same.

2. So when the status quo is altered or threatened, people take on different roles. Politics become a "game" we have to play in order to maintain the norm of what we are used to.

3. Many new officials run for office and pledge support for a certain policy. Eventually a resolution to implement a policy will be considered by a governance group. What will happen is that one official, we will call her Jane, will pledge support for a policy if another official, we will call him Jim, supports her policy. It's a game and sometimes the outcome is extremely positive and sometimes the outcome is negative.
(Second main point with support)

Connecting words or phrases: The two variables have been examined, so we have to answer the research question by looking at how they affect decision-making by congress.

III. By engaging in persuasive communication and playing the game of organizational politics, more power is gained by members of congress. Subsequently, decisions are being altered.
   A. Rather than voting based on one's belief, voting is often tainted by persuasive tactics because congressional members don't want to "rock the boat."
      1. Oftentimes, they want things to stay the same and they are resistant to change.
   B. Some members use persuasive tactics and engage in organizational politics with the "you scratch my back, I'll scratch yours" mentality in order to remain in congress.
      1. I'll vote for your bill because I know you'll vote for my bill shows little concern for the validity of the bill.
   C. So, decision-making in Congress appears to involve more than just making proposals and trying to persuade others to buy into certain ideas. It seems to also involve the manipulation of words and practices that causes one to promote or endorse legislation that one truly doesn't embrace.
      1. Of course, every member of Congress is not swayed by every persuasive tactic. However, research shows that many have utilized the two variables of persuasive communication and organizational politics, for personal gain.
      (Third main point with support)

CONCLUSION
   I. If members of organizations armed themselves with the positive tools of persuasion and accepted the reality that there are politics in every organization that they must encounter, then overall, they will be more empowered individuals in their respective fields.
   (Indicate the end)

   II. Today, we have examined persuasive communication and organizational politics by answering the question of how they influence decisions that are made by Congress?
   (Summarize your main points)

III. Individuals have their own political agendas but if members were to re-evaluate why they want to be in office from an altruistic standpoint, perhaps there would be less corruption. Or maybe this is a utopian ideal that will never be fully resolved. Zaleznick did say that organizations are political structures. Now, it seems that Congress is one of them and the stage is set ... for its exercise of power.
(Creative closures: emotional statements and a refer back to the intrigue)

OPEN FORUM

QUESTION 1: You stated that everyone uses persuasive communication at some point or another. Would you consider bribery a type of persuasive communication?

ANSWER 1: Well, yes. Essentially, bribery is the same as manipulation, and manipulation is a category of persuasive strategies that I discussed earlier.

QUESTION 2: Is there a theory of communication that would align with the research you have presented?

ANSWER 2: I am so glad you asked that! Actually, Irving Janis's Groupthink Theory ties in nicely with my research. Due to time constraints, I cannot elaborate on the theory. However, the underlying premise of the theory is that when working in a group, oftentimes group pressures cause members of the group to make faulty decisions. In my research, I used this theory to show how Congress (a group) can be influenced by those pressures.

April René Payne
Graduate Teaching Assistant
Department of Organizational Communication
Murray State University

A SAMPLE MANUSCRIPT OUTLINE

for

The Case Study

(Reviewing an Article or Case Study)

(WE LOVE FOOD, INC. PROMISES TO IMPROVE SAFETY RECORD)

(This is a fictitious organization and case study)

INTRODUCTION

I. Safety.
(Intrigue: emotional word)

II. This case study about We Love Food, Incorporated was created after my friend was injured at the Nashville plant. As an OSHA specialist, I wanted to impress upon this audience the importance of knowing the many violations we encounter so we can discuss how to minimize those violations across the country.

(Introduce the topic and tell why you are qualified to speak)

III. Safety violations affect our health and economy.

(Explain the benefits of listening)

IV. I'll give an overview of the company, point out the violations and what this company agreed to do to fix them, and then we'll allow for a discussion about possible solutions for companies like We Love Food, Inc.

(Preview the main points)

Connecting words or phrases: The company . . .

BODY

I. Wholesome Path manufactures organic whole grain foods. It started out as a very small company with about 12 people.

A. About four years after its conception, its leader, Lori Bee, took the small company public. It soon began growing at a very rapid pace. Throughout this high growth period, it has remained in touch with its all-natural organic roots and the people that work for the company.

B. Although the management was good at maintaining its food certifications, the administration was not knowledgeable about all of the safety regulations that govern the plant.

C. The employees told OSHA about the violations and how they felt their lives were in danger. OSHA maintains that its chief concern is to ensure that the workplace is safe for everyone who works at the plant or visits the premises.

(First main point with support)

Connecting words or phrases: The violations . . .

II. Worker training and safety programs at Wholesome Path's food processing plant were found to be below industry standards during the inspection.

A. Inspectors for OSHA identified more than 25 safety and health hazards at the plant during an inspection conducted during the last three months.

1. The agency cited Wholesome Path for:

a. Violating requirements for turning off machinery during maintenance and providing safeguards so they could not be restarted during maintenance (Lock-out Tag-Out)

b. Incomplete procedures for work performed in confined spaces including tanks and pits

c. Insufficient protective gear (lack of goggles, ear plugs, etc.)

d. Lack of training for forklift operators

       e. Failure to have safety rules posted

      (Second main point with support)

Connecting words or phrases: Despite the problems, changes will be made.

III. Plant manager Patsy Beamer said, "We are making the necessary changes to ensure that we comply with all regulations and protect our employees. We do believe that safety is paramount."

    A. Wholesome Path agreed to:

      1. Pay a $90,000 fine

      2. Put plant supervisors through more approved OSHA safety training

      3. Provide safety training for employees

      4. Make the workplace safer

      (Third main point with support)

CONCLUSION

   I. *We Love Food* wants to promote the highest standards in the food manufacturing industry.

   (Indicate the end)

  II. We know how they started and what areas they improved upon.

  (Summarize your main points)

 III. Hopefully one day, we specialists will see less OSHA recordables and more OSHA awards.

 (Creative closure: emotional statement)

OPEN FORUM

QUESTION 1: What might the company have done to prevent them from getting into trouble with OSHA?

ANSWER 1: More training is the key. Too many employees have basic training but they are not given several potential disasters to look at. There are always several ways to injure oneself. These need to be discussed and ways to avoid the disasters need to be discussed. It also won't hurt for companies to re-train employees twice a year so they don't forget procedures and preventative measures.

QUESTION 2: What can we recommend to ensure that training programs are adequate?

ANSWER 2: The best thing to do is track progress. Keep a record of excellence and record the names of those who trained those divisions. You can also check with the OSHA organization and ask for recommended training programs with high reputations for excellence.

QUESTION 3: What type of training could you provide for the supervisors and management, besides safety, that would help them comply with OSHA requirements?

ANSWER 3: Communication training would be beneficial. It's often overlooked because it's a "soft skill." However, the more professional one is in dealing with employees, the more likely the employee will listen to instructions and comply with requirements. Many employees are willing to comply with regulations but miss information during training because the speakers are too boring and the message is lost. There is a break in the retention which could cause the employee to do something wrong because he or she was mentally asleep during that part of the training. If you are going to supervise or train, you need to have a presentation that will be memorable especially since your life and the lives of others are at risk.

Coel Coleman

 ## THE ROAST

This is the consummate *After-Dinner* event involving several presentations. Most people in the audience know the roastee or someone connected to the roastee.

The contributor to this section has over thirty years of experience as a presenter in the fields of education, ministry and communication. Professional humorist Jerry W. Drye, M.S. explains this unique presentation over the next several pages. He allows us to grasp the dynamics of a roast through his tips and his sample manuscript.

Image © Katrina Brown, 2009. Used under license from Shutterstock, Inc.

Suggested Aids

- A large picture of the honoree that would be humorous but not offensive

- An object that represents that person's wonderful personality or achievements

tips Tips for a Successful Roast

Many people are familiar with roasts, having seen them on television. The Friar's Club has been conducting roasts for years and several cable channels have presented numerous roasts of celebrities. While these are excellent examples of the structure and format of a roast you should exercise extreme caution when hosting a roast for your organization.

Many businesses, non-profit institutions, service groups, and other organizations host roasts to raise funds and/or to honor some person in the organization or community. These can be great fun for all concerned but should differ distinctly from the roasts you see performed by professional performers in one important way. You should not skewer the guest of honor with ribald humor or mean-spirited remarks. The performers on television have "entertainment only" as their purpose. Your purpose is to provide gentle, good-natured ribbing to the person whom you are honoring. Do not, as they say in the world of comedy, "work blue." Keep your remarks wholesome and appropriate to the occasion.

A roast is usually associated with a dinner. As such, all of the presenters at the roast are considered after-dinner speakers. The goal is to keep things light and entertaining. There are two groups of people at a roast: The audience and the members of the dais. The audience may be comprised of members of the organization, others connected with the organization, community members, family members and friends of the honoree. The "dais" is the platform where the speakers will sit during the dinner and where the speakers will perform. It will usually have a lectern in the center with tables on either side where the presenters will be seated. Generally the guest of honor will be seated immediately to one side of the lectern and the master or mistress of ceremonies will be on the other side. The other speakers will fill out the rest of the seats at the table.

There are three kinds of speakers at the roast: The master or mistress of ceremonies (Roastmaster), the persons honoring the guest of honor (Roasters), and the guest of honor (Roastee). Each speaker has a very specific role.

Roastmaster

The roastmaster serves as the master or mistress of ceremonies. If you are selected as a roastmaster, you should have excellent presentation skills and some comedic timing. You should have a connection with the roastee and you should help the other speakers adhere to the schedule.

The roastmaster should:

- Make opening remarks welcoming the guests and describing the event

- Keep things moving and on time

- Work with each speaker about logistics (time limits, specific jokes, etc.)

- Determine the speaking order

- Introduce each roaster and the roastee

- Work with the guest of honor and the planning committee about what will transpire

- Close the event

Roasters

The speakers will make humorous and complimentary remarks about the guest of honor. If you are a roaster, take time to prepare so that your content is humorous but sincere and captivating.

The roaster should:

- Give amusing but tasteful anecdotes about the person being honored

- Focus on the relationship with the roastee

- Remember the goal is not to embarrass the honoree but to celebrate the person and his/her accomplishments

- Make brief humorous comments about one or two of the other roasters but the focus should be on the roastee

- Be brief, light-hearted, and end with some very positive remarks about the guest of honor

Roastee

The roastee is the honoree. If you are chosen to be the roastee, you are already well-respected and loved. Remember this as you give your presentation.

The roastee should:

- Be gracious

- Make amusing and appreciative remarks about the roasters, organizational leaders, and guests

- Have the longest single speech but still keep things relatively brief depending on the nature of the event especially if there are other elements to the program besides the roast (although having "other elements" is not recommended)

The simple acronym **R.O.A.S.T.** may help you to remember the following:

Rehearsal   It is very important for each speaker to have a well-prepared speech that he or she has practiced a few times. "Winging it" is not a recommended practice. It shows disrespect to the guest of honor and to the audience. Remember the old joke about the visitor to New York who asked a traffic cop how to get to Carnegie Hall? The officer replied: "Practice, practice, practice."

Originality	Make every attempt to present material that is fresh and original. Remember to focus on the roastee, the roastee's position within the organization, and the roastee's relationship with you and the other members of the dais.
Amusing	Avoid being overly sentimental or serious. Keep most of the comments light. Speakers in these instances will often use stale old jokes that have been heard time and time again. If you choose to use standard jokes from the public domain you should do two things: make certain that no other speaker is going to use the same jokes; and personalize the jokes to make members of the dais or organization actual characters in the joke. If you are not a professional comedian or comedy writer, it may be better to tell amusing stories from your relationship with the honoree. Humorous observations, top ten lists, and light verse might also be appropriate and fairly easy to develop.
Sensitive	Be sensitive to the honoree and his or her family. Do not try to embarrass the roastee. Again, remember that the television roasts are not the models for you to follow. Your purpose is to honor and celebrate. Be sensitive to all guests and audience members. I was asked once to speak for an organization after its leader heard me at another event. I had told several humorous stories about the births of our two children. The person who invited me to speak told me before the event that a member of their organization had recently suffered a miscarriage. I was glad to get this information. I was able to edit my presentation so I didn't make that audience member uncomfortable. Avoid racist, sexist, and demeaning language at all times.
Time	Stay within your time limits. These will be determined beforehand but a good general rule is to have each speaker talk for about 3 to 5 minutes with the guest of honor speaking about 10 to 15 minutes. (Meeting planners can work out specific times with the roastmaster). Remember the old show business axiom: "Always leave them wanting more."

A successful roast takes a lot of planning and hard work but it can be a very enjoyable and meaningful event for all concerned.

A SAMPLE MANUSCRIPT

for

The Roast

(Including speeches from the roastmaster, roasters and roastee)

The following is an original fictional roast. It is meant to give an example of the format and flow of an actual roast. The characters and the event are not real.

SCENARIO: Rod Johnson began working for the Rubber Chicken Soup Company (manufacturers of novelty items) right out of college. He has worked his way up to the position of Vice President of Marketing. He has recently turned 70. This roast will celebrate his fifty years with the company and his pending retirement. Among the roasters are his administrative assistant Rose Carter, the shipping and receiving manager Mervyn Sprogminster, and Rod's wife Margie. The roastmaster is Jack Barran, the president of the company.

ROASTMASTER: Good evening ladies and gentlemen. We are here this evening to honor a legend in our company and in the industry. Rod Johnson has worked for this company for fifty years. Recently, someone informed me that he had just turned seventy. I remember being surprised about that. I thought to myself, "Rod is only seventy?"

Rod started out years ago as a production assistant. He has worked in every department in this company. Apparently, he wore out his welcome in each and every one of them. Rod has been a fixture in this company for a half a century. After awhile fixtures must be changed. However, we are not asking Rod to retire. He has helped this company become what it is today. Our success is his success. We thought it was only proper that since he has done so much to help our business grow, we should give him the business tonight. To help us do that, here are three people who know him very well.

Our first speaker knows Rod very well. Rose Carter has been Rod's administrative assistant for the last twenty-two years. She has been his right arm all that time . . . which is good because as you know, Rod is left-handed.

ROASTER ROSE: Thanks Jack. I am delighted to be here to honor my boss. I have had many bosses over the years. I have had good bosses and bad bosses. And then there is Rod. How can I rank him among the bosses I have had? Of all the bosses I have ever had, Rod is the most . . . recent. Actually, the boss I had before I came to work here made me not want to ever have another one. Rod was the closest thing to not having a boss I could find so I came to work here.

In the twenty-two years I have worked here, I have rarely seen Rod (turns to the honoree) . . . nice to meet you. Rod has always remembered my birthday and the anniversary of my first day working here. He never acknowledged them in any special way but he remembered them. Actually, he would tell me: "Rose, send yourself something nice." Since this is the last year he can say that to me, I think I will send myself something really nice. I am sending me to Hawaii.

Rod, it has taken me twenty-two years to break you in and train you and now you are leaving me. Thank you for hiring me and making the last two decades the best years of my professional life. Enjoy your retirement with Margie. See me later and I will give you the dates of her birthday and anniversary.

ROASTMASTER: Thanks Rose. There should be a special award for you for having to put up with Rod all of these years. Our next presenter is a man who always has a clipboard in his hand. It makes him look like he is working. Welcome shipping and receiving manager, Mervyn Sprogminster.

ROASTER MERVYN: We have come this evening to honor one of the great men of industry. I think about some of the great pioneers and innovators of the past and think it's appropriate that we add the name of Rod Johnson to the list. Think about it. Johannes Gutenberg gave us movable type. Henry Ford gave us mass production. Eli Whitney gave us the cotton gin. And what of Rod Johnson? Rod Johnson has kept the world supplied with joy buzzers, exploding cigars, and whoopee cushions. Aren't you proud Rod? What a legacy. Someone notify the Nobel Prize committee.

When I think of Rod my back hurts. It hurts first of all because I carried him all these years. It hurts also because due to him we sent out more product than any other novelty company on planet earth. Thanks for the job security Rod, and for being a super person to work with. I hope the next seventy years are better than the last.

ROASTMASTER: Our last presenter knows Rod better than anyone. She has been married to him for nearly forty years. We should really be giving her an award for that. Ladies and gentlemen, Margie Johnson.

ROASTER MARGIE: Every day for the last forty years I have watched Rod leave the house and come to work here at the Rubber Chicken Soup Company. Soon he will not be leaving the house. I just wanted to say to Jack and everyone here at Rubber Chicken Soup . . . Thanks, thanks a lot. I cannot begin to tell you what a joy it is to know that I get to see him day in and day out . . . every minute of every day . . . from here on out. I have just one question . . . Could I have a job please? I will do anything as long as it gets me out of the house!

Now Rod is a great guy and a wonderful husband but not really the sharpest tool in the drawer. He asked me what I wanted to do now that he had extra time on his hands. I told him I had always wanted to take a trip around the world. He said: "Oh honey, let's go somewhere else." You see what I have to look forward to for years to come? Tonight, many of you have given testimonies about Rod's work habits. I just want you to know something. If you think he worked hard here, wait until I get him home. I love you Rod. See you at the house.

ROASTMASTER: Thanks Margie, our thoughts and prayers are with you. Now for the man of the hour. For fifty years he has truly been the face, heart, and conscience of this company. Here he is . . . Rod Johnson.

ROASTEE ROD: Ladies and gentlemen, I do not know when I have had an evening this enjoyable. I believe it was the night my appendix burst. Now, I know how folks at this company really feel about me. To my friends and co-workers Rose Carter and Mervyn Sprogminster, I just want to say this: Monday morning when you come to work I want you to think about me. I will be thinking about you. I will see your faces and I want you to see mine . . . thumbing my nose at you while you work and I fish.

Mervyn and Rose are two of the many reasons that this company is as successful as it is. Jack Barran is another. Jack has always had an open door policy. He always kept the door to his office open and a trail of jelly beans leading to it just so he could find his way back. Jack, and Rose, and Mervyn are not only great people to work with, they are great friends. I will miss you all.

But I am looking forward to spending more time with Margie, though it sounds like I am going to be very busy. Maybe you really could find her a job. The other day I asked Margie if after forty years of marriage she really loved me or just tolerated me. She did not even have to think about it. She said, "Rod, if I didn't love you, I couldn't tolerate you." Margie, thanks for loving and tolerating me. I love you too.

Thanks to everyone at the Rubber Chicken Soup Company for fifty great years. Someone once said that if you get a job you love, you will never have to work a day in your life. That is the way I feel about my work here. I have loved every minute of it. Thanks to the planning committee who put this together. Thanks to all of my co-workers, family members and friends. God bless you all. If you are ever around the house . . . drop in.

ROASTMASTER: Rod, no one deserves an evening like this more than you. Before we go I would like to make an announcement. As many of you know, Rod is a graduate and supporter of our local institution of higher learning Williams College. In your honor and in your name, the Rubber Chicken Soup Company is establishing an annual scholarship to Williams. Your generosity and good name will have a lasting impact on many lives for years to come. Thanks to everyone who helped to make this night possible. Travel home safely . . . good night.

Roast tips and manuscript submitted by:
Jerry W. Drye, M.S.
Humorist and Educator
Lecturer of Communication Studies
Clemson University

THE SALES PITCH

Just the word "sales" will cause some people to either get excited or uncomfortable. Therefore, assuring people that you won't pressure them or guilt them into buying something will serve in your favor. Tell the features of what you're selling, be knowledgeable and sincere. Those things will work more than high pressure sales' tactics.

Image © JupiterImages Corp., 2009.

A sales pitch requires composure, excellent eye contact, knowledge of what you are selling and a manuscript outline that is organized and persuasive.

If the audience invited you to speak, you will have a better chance of persuading the potential buyer. Make sure that people with the authority to buy what you are selling, are in the audience. Do not waste your time presenting for an audience of people who don't have the power to make a decision.

Sales presentations can vary in time and location. Some are time share presentations that take place all day and over a weekend and some are one minute television spots for some product that costs $19.95. Always be ready for audience members who are hostile, apathetic, fatigued or leery of your presentation regardless of how organized you are.

The Sales Pitch is pure persuasion. The following manuscript outline is a basic outline but you can also try the Monroe's Motivated Sequence: Gaining attention, showing a need for a change in the product or service, satisfying the need through the solution of buying what you're selling, stating through visualization all the wonderful things that will happen if the product/service is bought and then calling the potential buyer into action by asking him or her to actually make the purchase. A problem-solution pattern can also be effective. Explain the problems and then offer your solutions.

A sales presentation must be well-prepared! There is no way you can convince people to believe in what you pitch unless you have your points clear and organized. Make sure you explain that your product or service will meet a great need that the buyer may have. Practice strong facial expressions. Smile and frown. Make your face convey concern for the potential buyer not having your product or service. Also, show excitement for being able to offer the buyer what you have in your possession.

Suggested Aids

Obviously, you need to show whatever you are selling! You can:

- Have the actual object you are selling
- Have a chart or graph showing how the product has influenced a group of people over a period of time
- Have pictures of those affected by the product or service
- Have large red numbers or large words in dark ink professionally printed on poster boards if you wish to emphasize statistics or key words

A SAMPLE MANUSCRIPT OUTLINE
for
The Sales Pitch

INTRODUCTION

I. If you want to be abused come to the front of the room.
(Intrigue: emotional statement)

II. No one came forward and yet I know through statistical data, that more than a third of the 100 young ladies in this room, are abused or have been abused. One third have not been abused but know people who have been abused; and the other women are potential victims especially if they don't think they are. I have been a Visa College Representative for two years and I used to be a victim of domestic abuse.
(Introduce the topic and tell why you are qualified to speak)

III. You can close your ears and your minds but don't close your hearts or someone you love may suffer or die at the hands of someone they know. I'm here to ask your sorority to purchase at least $10,000 worth of visa gift cards. With each card you buy, half of that purchase amount will be donated to the *STOP THE VIOLENCE* campaign. The money goes to help abuse victims throughout the country.
(Explain the benefits of listening)

IV. I'll explain what the card is, how it helps to save lives and why your sorority should make this purchase.
(Preview the main points)

Connecting words or phrases: So what is this visa card?

BODY

I. The visa card is a gift card and there are three different amounts.
  A. There is a $25, $50 and $100 card.
   1. Each card can be used just like any visa card.
      a. You can purchase gas, food, clothing, etc.
      b. Just activate the card through the 800 number and it's ready to be used!
  B. The more expensive the card, the more money is donated.
   1. Five dollars for every $25 card goes to the fund.
   2. Ten dollars is donated for every $50 card.
   3. And twenty-five dollars from every $100 card will go to help the victims.
      (First main point with support)

Connecting words or phrases: So, how do you know that this purchase will save lives?

II. Our company will send you proof every quarter of how your contributions have helped to save lives.
   A. Shelters are primarily run by volunteers so the money is not going into pockets.
      1. The money is going to feed and clothe those who had to run away in the middle of the night with young children.
      2. The money is used to make sure the heat and water bills are paid.
      3. The money is used to help educate the children within shelter walls so their education doesn't suffer.
   B. You will get a statement in the mail from our accounting department which is in great standing with rating companies.
      1. You will see which city shelter receives your money each quarter.
      2. You will also see what supplies are funded through your contributions.
      3. If you ever need to question an expense, our accountants will answer your questions and send you proof that's approved by the government.
      (Second main point with support)

Connecting words or phrases: Your sorority has won awards for philanthropy.

III. Delta Alpha Zeta Sigma is known to be a sorority that gives back to the community.
   A. I realize that you support cancer research, the children's hospital and the local Needline.
      1. These are all excellent fundraising endeavors.
   B. However, most of these involve solicitations from other people.
      1. The *Stop The Violence Visa* is a personal contribution that you give in which you actually receive an emotional *and* financial benefit.
         a. You don't lose any money because the $50 you give to pay for the $50 card goes directly into your pocket through your purchases of things you wish to buy.
         b. The wonderful part is knowing that your fifty dollars will yield a contribution to help victims of abuse. You just can't lose and you win any way you look at it.
         (Third main point with support)

CONCLUSION
   I. Delta Alpha Zeta Sigma has a long history of giving and we wanted your tradition to be further enriched through our great fundraising option.
      (Indicate the end)

   II. What better way to serve humankind than to save lives through our visa?
      (Summarize your main points)

   III. I want you to come to the front of the room . . . but don't come to the front because you're abused . . . come to the front of the room because you believe that violence can be healed through the *Stop the Violence Visa.*
      (Creative closure: refer back to the intrigue)

Coel Coleman

THE TEAM SYMPOSIUM

The symposium is similar to the panel discussion. Both are team presentations. They both have moderators who introduce the topic, discussion and participants. They both usually have a forum after the presentation.

Tyler, Kristin and Luke prepare for a team symposium for class.

The primary difference between the symposium and the panel discussion is that a symposium requires short prepared speeches and a panel discussion is a discussion with back and forth dialogue and feedback. Each speaker for a symposium gives an individual short speech about an aspect of the topic. Then, a question and answer forum will follow. There may be some dialogue among the team members in a symposium but the symposium is used as a means for an entire team to present information to an audience. The purpose is not to have a discussion among themselves.

Symposiums are used for public relations, campaigns, team sales lectures, etc. Each speaker for a symposium should have a typed presentation outline in a portfolio. Memorization is fine but it's dangerous. If one person loses his or her memory, the entire team could be at risk for looking unprepared. Know your presentation. Each team member should memorize his or her introduction and conclusion; but it's not necessary to memorize entire speeches! Each person should still have a typed presentation outline with the main points and quotations.

Suggested Aids

The trend is the use of PowerPoint and multimedia devices. This is fine but please don't abuse the technology. An entire presentation with PowerPoint slides is quite uncreative although overly utilized. It's best to use several types of aids especially for a sales/public relations' symposium. Showing a potential buyer that your team is versatile and flexible will be an advantage over a team that spends the entire presentation reading off a screen and pushing a remote control.

- Five to eight PowerPoint slides with pictures that are colorful and that emphasize your message, i.e., the living room, bedroom and bathroom of the time-share you are trying to sell

- An object like a stuffed animal to show how your charity should be supported because so many children go without basic toys each year

- A pictogram that shows how student enrollment has increased in the area of Occupational Safety and Health Administration

A SAMPLE MANUSCRIPT
for
The Team Symposium

INTRODUCTION

PERSON A: We will not sell you anything!
(Intrigue: emotional statement)

PERSON B: However, since you are approaching your sophomore year, and you are still undecided about a major, we wanted to inform you about the jobs you can get with a degree in organizational communication and why employers are drawn to graduates of this program.
(Introduce the topic)

PERSON C: The four of us have worked well together for three weeks to prepare and we decided that we don't want a hostile audience. So, you won't be subjected to high pressure tactics!
(Tell why you are qualified to speak and the benefits of listening)

MODERATOR: I'm person D, your moderator. Person A will explain what you will encounter as an organizational communication major; Person B will tell you about the various jobs our graduates have; Person C will explain why employers are hiring our students over some other students who are in degree specific fields and I will . . . relax.
(Preview the main points)

MODERATOR: Person A . . . don't you have something to say?

BODY

PERSON A: I certainly do. So you want to know what you can do with a degree that doesn't require you to sit for a state exam or collect 30 apprentice hours before actually getting a paycheck? Well, organizational communication teaches theories and skills that allow you to do anything. You will learn management techniques, leadership, training, presentation, and negotiation skills. You will learn how to handle conflict in the workplace or at any organization. You will learn strategies to effectively increase employee morale that should lead to an increase in productivity regardless of where you work. This is not a major for students who enjoy reading and listening to hour long lectures and then taking exams all semester. This major is for students who like to read, listen and then immediately apply what they have learned through individual and team projects. With this major, you have information and applications. Remember that.

MODERATOR: Remember that. Person B don't you have something to say?

PERSON B: I certainly do. So you want to know what you can do with a degree in Organizational Communication? Our graduates are lawyers, Washington D.C. government officials, bank vice-presidents, professors, corporate trainers, human resource directors, business owners, ministers, executive directors for non-profit organizations, and the list goes on. We give you information about how to create strong relationships between employers and employees. We try to enhance your written and oral presentation skills. It doesn't matter what company you want to work for or what specific title you want to have. What matters is that you will be able to navigate through any training program for any company while having the special skills to help a company foster a healthier work environment. With this major, you can do anything! Remember that.

MODERATOR: Remember that. Person C . . . You have something to say too?

PERSON C: I certainly do. So you want to know why some employers specifically ask for our students? It's simple. Many graduates leave with the basic skills and knowledge about their respective fields. However, despite core knowledge, these students lack communication skills necessary to enhance employee morale. Many businesses are not as successful as they should be because employee morale is low or effective management practices are ignored or forgotten. Many companies want fresh ideas about how to solve problems and increase morale. This major teaches numerous theories about organizational structures and superior-subordinate relationships. Many companies would rather hire our students and give them company training rather than hire people who understand company policies but who lack an understanding of leadership principles, interpersonal communication and team dynamics. With this major, you dictate where you go and you can go anywhere. You're never stuck doing the same job because your skills and experiences are transferable. Remember that.

CONCLUSION

MODERATOR: There's a lot to remember!
(Indicate the end)

You learn; you apply what you learn; you graduate with skills that are needed for every profession.

(Summarize your main points)

So if nothing else . . . remember that.

(Creative closure: emotional statement)

OPEN FORUM

QUESTION: Does your department help us to find jobs?

ANSWER: Yes. We post internship and job announcements. Many of our alumni call and request our students because they know the quality of education you will receive since they went through the program too.

QUESTION: Can you make a lot of money with this degree?

ANSWER: Well, as you heard, the jobs are quite diverse and several are considered high paying jobs. Most of our graduates don't start making $40 or $50 thousand a year but most wind up making that and much more within a few years of graduation.

Coel Coleman

 # THE TOAST

If coherent, the audience will be thrilled to hear you speak! However, they will want you to be sentimental, brief and prepared. If you throw something together, the listeners won't be upset but they may talk about you on their way home.

Toasts are social and business celebrations. The time of day is irrelevant and the location doesn't matter either. Sincerity is paramount.

You don't have to rehearse a lot. However, you do need to know what you will say. You don't need a presentation outline but you should create a manuscript outline and be familiar with the organization of your presentation. If you stumble a lot, your own credibility will be affected and if you are at a business function, you could potentially embarrass yourself and your employer and co-workers.

Professor Patty S. Parish, M.S. has spent years educating students. Also, she and her husband are ministers who attend a lot of functions that require giving toasts. Her sample outline serves as a guide for those who wish to honor people with an organized and respectful toast presentation.

Suggested Aids

- A raised glass with a beverage in it
- A raised candle for a moment of silence or to light the room

---

A SAMPLE MANUSCRIPT OUTLINE
for
The Toast

(The following is a fictitious Toast)

(WEDDING)

INTRODUCTION

I. Jacob and Lindsey are truly a storybook couple! My name is John and I have been given the great honor of giving this toast. I have been close friends with Jacob for many years and I have had the good fortune to watch the love between Jacob and Lindsey blossom and grow into something special. Tonight, we have gathered to celebrate that love.
(Intrigue: emotional statement and why you are qualified to speak)

II. First of all, I would like to thank you on behalf of Jacob and Lindsey for coming and being a part of this very special night in their lives. Their joy and happiness is made complete by your presence tonight.
(Thank everyone for being a part of the celebration.)

III. Let's toast their fairy tale and their love.
(Preview the main points)

BODY

I. Jacob and Lindsey's relationship is truly one from the pages of a storybook.
  A. From the moment they met . . . that first glance from across the room . . . they knew that they were meant to be together. I was there and witnessed that glance!
  B. Their love is also like a fairy tale because they bring so much joy to each other every moment they are together. From the first time they were together, they found they had so much in common from baseball to a love of classical music.
  (First main point with support)

Connecting words or phrases: Their love deserves to have this toast.

I. Let's raise our glasses and toast this special couple.
  A. Jacob and Lindsey, we toast you and your love. May your love always be like the sun . . . there to warm your days.

B. May your love always be like the stars . . . there to enchant your nights.

C. May your love always be like the moon . . . there to smile on all your hopes and dreams

D. Together . . . you're a dream come true.

    (Second main point with support)

CONCLUSION

  I. To Jacob and Lindsey . . .

    (Indicate the end)

  II. We salute your fairy tale which is your love!

    (Summarize your main points)

 III. We love you . . . cheers! Always remember what Elizabeth Browning said about love. "Love does not make the world go 'round; love is what makes the ride worthwhile."

    (Creative closures: emotional statements and a quotation)

Manuscript outline submitted by:
Patty S. Parish, M.S.
Organizational Communication Lecturer
Murray State University

THE TOUR

If this is a school or workplace tour, most audience members will be interested in seeing the operations so you shouldn't have a hostile audience. The audience could include company officials, local business people, or school children.

If you conduct a tour for some entertainment purpose, your audience will either be excited to be at your location or exhausted because they have been touring different facilities all day. All audiences will expect an entertaining lecture with short sentences and plenty of time for questions.

If you must have a presentation outline, make sure it's in a solid color folder and it's typed. This is the one presentation in which an index card can be used. However, regardless of what is used, make sure the print is typed and NOT hand-written! Hand-written notes reflect poorly on your company and on your ability to be professional.

This is a short presentation with A LOT of impromptu elements. However, you still need to practice an opening and a closing. As long as you know the main areas you will be touring, the body of the message doesn't have to be scripted. However, the introduction and conclusion should be written and rehearsed before the tour presentation.

Image © Natalia Bratslavsky, 2009. Used under license from Shutterstock, Inc.

Suggested Aids

- A company uniform

- A gift at the end of the tour like a coffee mug, with a label of the school on it

---

A SAMPLE MANUSCRIPT OUTLINE

for

The Tour

(CAMPUS TOUR)

(All names and situations are fictitious)

INTRODUCTION

I. Anthony J. D'Angelo in the College Blue Book said, "Without a sense of caring, there can be no sense of community." In the next thirty to forty minutes, I will take you through key areas on campus.
(Intrigue: quotation)

II. If you have questions along the way, keep them in your memory bank and several times during this tour, we will take a break and I'll entertain your questions. I've been doing this tour since sophomore year and I love meeting new people and sharing what I know about this great university.
(Introduce the topic and tell why you are qualified to speak)

III. Hopefully when you leave today, you will have a better understanding of who we are and what we can do for you!
(Explain the benefits of listening)

IV. So first, I'll share some history as we walk by the administrative buildings; secondly, I'll show you the key academic college buildings; and finally, we'll see the student center and recreation areas. Later today, the housing department will show you the dorms.
(Preview the main points)

Connecting words or phrases: So when was Technology Tech built?

BODY

I. Tech was the vision of David Darryl Duane. He was born in the suburbs of Baltimore, Maryland.

    A. As a teenager, he created several products for class projects.

        1. As an adult he decided to sell the products to local businesses.

        2. When his cameras kept selling, he realized that he had products that people wanted.

    B. He also noticed that people wanted to learn his trade.

        1. He started teaching out of his home and then got the funding to open his first building in downtown Baltimore.

        2. As the business expanded, he bought more land and buildings were built.

    C. This building was the first to house the administrative offices.

        1. Now, it has been remodeled. The president and her cabinet have offices in David Darryl Duane Hall.

    D. This tall white building to the left is where many of you will run if you have any problems with scheduling, grades, financial aid or admissions.

        1. This is where you will go to pay any parking tickets; or if you want a job at Tech, the HR Department is on the 4th floor.
        (First main point with support)

Connecting word or phrase: Are there any questions so far? Now that you know where to go if you have issues, let's go down this sidewalk and glance at the academic colleges.

II. Here are the colleges . . .

    A. The College of Education is the first building on your left.

        1. It's housed in Louvania Hall named after a prominent Maryland educator.

    B. Right behind Education is the College of Engineering and Science.

        1. There are over ten majors from chemistry to computer technology and electronics.

    C. The third college is the College of Business which is right there to the right.

        1. You will find the accounting, marketing, communication and management departments in this college.
        (Second main point with support)

Connecting word or phrase: So we know the people who do a lot of paperwork but where do you get to unwind and have fun?

I. Let's keep walking and when we get to the top of the hill we'll stop and rest at the Student Center.

    A. The Erica Tiffany Danielle Center has four eating places, two banquet rooms, meeting rooms, and the Devin Campus Store.

    B. Outside this back door, you can see a practice field, and the basketball and tennis courts.

    C. You can't see them from here but an outdoor swimming pool, a football field and a track are located over that hill.

    (Third main point with support)

CONCLUSION

I. Are there any final questions about Technology Tech?
(Indicate the end)

II. You now know a little history about our university, our academics and our activities.
(Summarize your main points)

III. I hope you enjoyed the tour; are there any questions? (FORUM)

    A. If you did enjoy the tour today, why not join our caring community at Technology Tech and be the focus of a lot of love and respect?

    (Creative closures: direct and rhetorical questions)

Coel Coleman

 # THE TRIBUTE

With the exception of on-site employees, most guests will know the honoree. Both genders are usually represented and the audience will reflect the occasion involving employment, family, community, etc. Regardless, the language in your message should be vivid and emotional to evoke a great love and remembrance of that person or concept.

Your delivery is so important if you pay tribute. A lackluster performance will minimize that person's achievements or that concept's power. You must have vocal variety and varied facial expressions. Sometimes tributes involve the media so be aware of any electronic devices and

make sure you stand close enough to be heard and far enough away so that you don't sound like you are screaming into the microphone.

Suggested Aids

- A very large picture of the honoree but make sure it is tasteful, colorful and attractive

- A musical slideshow of memorable times in the life of the honoree

- Party favors and streamers at the end of your presentation to indicate a great celebration of the achievements of whatever or whomever you are celebrating

---

A SAMPLE MANUSCRIPT OUTLINE
for
The Tribute

INTRODUCTION

I. It appeared to be an ordinary Fourth of July Celebration. But when he walked onto the stage, I noticed that he had the most amazing smile on his face and his skin was beautiful. I sat quietly as he spoke of his experiences during the Iraq War. He had lost his arm; he had lost his leg; he had lost his ability to dress himself in the morning. But as he spoke words of encouragement and wisdom and thankfulness, I noticed that he had not lost the one thing I took for granted each day . . . joy. He had not lost that inner peace . . . that inner joy.
(Intrigue: short story)

II. I needed to share that I heard his testimony because we honor so many who have lost their lives. Today, we celebrate the strength of those who are left behind and the family members who love them. I have so many friends who have shared their pain with me. I know the pain is real.
(Introduce the topic and tell why you are qualified to speak)

III. So many of us have suffered a loss and even if we don't have a loved one in the Iraq War, we have battles we fight each day at work and in our homes.
(Explain the benefits of listening)

IV. A few minutes doesn't do them justice but I hope to give a glimpse of how much we appreciate who they are and who they will become.
(Preview the main points)

Connecting words or phrases: They leave home knowing who they represent.

BODY

  I. United States Soldiers are special people. Soldiers know who they are. They are those willing to fight for humankind and for the goals set forth by our leaders.

  A. They may be fearful, excited or confused, but regardless, they know that they will go out and defend democracy and freedom.

Connecting words or phrases: United States soldiers are amazing people.

  II. Soldiers know they will become role models for so many who hear their stories or watch them live their lives.

  A. Those sitting with us tonight know that their experiences are a part of history that may be painful and yet liberating.

CONCLUSION

  I. The war rages on . . . but so does the courage.
  (Indicate the end)

  II. So many are no longer with us and we grieve for their absence. But those who are still on this earth, sitting in this room, and watching through that camera . . . they are special and amazing because of who they are and who they will become.
  (Summarize your main points)

  III. We always honor the deceased but tonight we stand and salute the living souls and their families; we salute them for their strength; we salute them for their courage; we salute them for their love. Thank you United States soldiers and thank you family members for helping to keep their spirits high!
  (Creative closures: emotional statements)

Coel Coleman

THE WELCOME AND RESPONSE

A welcome and a response should be brief and organized. If done well, both speakers will evoke excitement for the event that is to follow. Both should be rehearsed a few times so that you don't stumble and make the occasion seem frivolous. The welcome and subsequent response do not need aids because they are both very brief. If you use a presentation aid, it should enhance the enthusiasm of the

event and it should be large enough for everyone to see. For example, I could say, "A toast to you, let's enjoy the evening in style." Then, I could raise a champagne glass. The response should acknowledge the person who gave the welcome and the comments that were made during the welcome. One reflects the other. There should be an element of continuity.

Suggested Aids

None are needed for these two very short presentations.

A SAMPLE MANUSCRIPT OUTLINE
for
The Welcome

INTRODUCTION
I. Dreams do come true!
(Intrigue: emotional statement)

II. Welcome to a night of dreams. On behalf of the entire executive council of the Student Leaders in America, I am honored to welcome you to a night of music, testimonies, and fellowship.
(Introduce the topic and preview the main activities)

Connecting words or phrases: Dreams . . .

BODY
I. Tonight you don't have to worry about working; we'll start the music for you.
(First main point)

II. You don't have to worry about what you say; we'll have the speakers do the talking.
(Second main point)

III. You don't have to worry about being alone or being lonely; we'll have a warm smile and a strong embrace.
(Third main point)

CONCLUSION
I. We have love for your presence and respect for your differences.
(Indicate the end)

II. We are thrilled you came to share the melodies, the memories, and the miracles.
(Summarize your main points)

III. Welcome and enjoy us as much as we enjoy you! Enjoy the dream tonight!
   (Creative closure: emotional statement)

Coel Coleman

A SAMPLE MANUSCRIPT OUTLINE
for
The Response

INTRODUCTION

  I. There were flat tires, family illness and some of us are: "direction challenged" when it comes to reading a map! But we made it here through a miracle! We dreamed about this for a long time.
  (Intrigue: emotional statements)

  II. Caroline, thank you for that beautiful welcome. We come from so many different districts. However, despite our differences, we have one dream in common: the ability to be a part of this fine organization that promotes leadership and ethical business practices.
  (Introduce the topic and preview the main points)

Connecting words or phrases: We've learned so much about leadership skills.

BODY

  I. Whether we attend workshops or read texts, we have learned valuable skills.
  (First main point)

Connecting words or phrases: We've embraced ethics and integrity when conducting negotiations and employee interviews.

  II. We now know it's not just what you do but how you do it.
  (Second main point)

CONCLUSION

  I. Again, we accept your welcome.
  (Indicate the end)

  II. We thank you for the leadership and the knowledge.
  (Summarize your main points)

  III. Please know that we feel the sincerity of your welcome, the warmth of your smile, and the strength of your embrace.
  (Creative closure: emotional statement)

Coel Coleman

THE WORKSHOP/SEMINAR

With this presentation, you act as a facilitator who introduces the topic area and controls the discussion and/or activities. The biggest difference between the workshop and the seminar is the interaction. The seminar may or may not include individual or team activities. The workshop has some type of hands-on activity. You must keep the audience engaged and active in some way. Most seminars and workshops are a part of conferences or retreats.

A good workshop/seminar lecture still requires organization from the introduction to the forum. DON'T FORGET: When you act as a facilitator at a workshop/seminar, you will have a closure at the end of your lecture and then a second closure after the forum of questions and answers. Never leave an audience wondering what will happen next or whether the workshop/seminar is finally over. It's YOUR job to make sure the structure is clear and unambiguous.

Suggested Aids

- A package of handouts but make sure people don't read ahead. Guide the audience to each page and remind them to turn the package over when you want them to just listen to you speak

- A few PowerPoint slides of pictures that aid your topic

- PowerPoint slides of bullets of main points but make sure you still have color, a picture, and at least a 24-point font

- Candy is good but make it have a purpose; i.e., tootsie pops to show how we are different on the outside but the same on the inside; chocolate kisses symbolizing the need to love ourselves each day; potato chips and pretzels to show how two different ideas born from two different places can work together effectively

A SAMPLE MANUSCRIPT OUTLINE

for

The Workshop

INTRODUCTION

I. Everyone stand up. Now sit down. Stand up. Sit down. Stand up one more time. Sit down. **(Intrigue: emotional statements and actions)**

II. That was annoying huh? Conflict. Whether constructive or destructive, it can be annoying and sometimes exhausting. Thank you for listening to me and following directions despite being annoyed because listening and following directions are the core of today's workshop. I'm Colleen Bloodworth and it's a joy to lead this very important mission to assist you with mediation as a means of conflict resolution. **(Introduction of the topic and the facilitator)**

III. This workshop is designed to enhance your ability to resolve conflict among your team members. Less conflict . . . more cohesion . . . more cohesion . . . more positive results. **(Explain the benefits of listening)**

IV. We are going to examine mediation by defining the process, looking at the mediator's role and then we will break into teams and practice mock mediations. **(Preview the main points.)**

BODY

I. Mediation is a form of alternative dispute resolution that involves two or more people trying to reach a mutual agreement.

Most seminars are heavily lecture-based while most workshops involve audience activities.

A. It's important to first define the problem. Make sure the overall problem is agreed upon. This way, everyone is clear about the dispute. Make sure all parties agree to a good faith effort to reach an agreement.

B. Allow all parties involved to talk. There should be no disrespectful language or any interruptions.

C. Reach an agreement through helping the parties to brainstorm for solutions to the problem.

D. Implement the agreement by having both parties sign a contract stating that a good faith effort will be made to honor all promises that are made during the mediation. If possible, have everyone sign a written contract for future reference should anything precipitate court proceedings.

(First main point with support)

Connecting words and phrases: A mediator is a liaison.

II. The mediator's role is one of a neutral position.
   A. You can't take sides and call yourself an effective mediator. Someone will notice the bias and the mediation effort will fail. You have to be honest and genuine in wanting all parties to resolve the problem.
   B. It's the mediator's role to introduce the process and make sure that both parties understand each person will get to state his or her grievance without being interrupted.
   (Second main point with support)

Connecting words and phrases: The overall process and your role as a mediator are not difficult in theory. The challenge is remembering to follow the directions that were given today and being able to guide the process with professionalism and sincerity.

III. Let's count off into fours and break into our teams.
   A. Once seated, have one person come and get the case scenario and mediation guideline sheet.
   B. Two people will be the mediators and two will be the actors. Don't be melodramatic or you'll spend too much time laughing and not concentrating. (Smiles)

(Breakout Sessions: Case Scenarios)

(Third main point with support)

CONCLUSION
I. Are there any final questions?
   (Indicate the end)

II. I can't change whether you choose to implement what was taught today; but I can leave knowing that you know a little more about mediation and the role of a mediator.
   (Summarize your main points)

III. If you need more information, you can access my website at bestfacilitator.com. It's all about being the best employer you can be … who wouldn't want to be the best?
   (Creative closures: emotional statement and a rhetorical question)

Coel Coleman

CHAPTER

8

A Quick Impromptu Guide

In keeping with the name it represents, this will be a quick chapter guide. If you have to speak with little or no preparation, here is a four step process:

Step 1: Intrigue the audience

Step 2: State two or three short main points

Step 3: Support the main points with brief statistics, examples, stories or testimonies

Step 4: Summarize and close

Image © Attsetski, 2009. Used under license from Shutterstock, Inc.

SAMPLE MANUSCRIPT OUTLINE

(name is fictitious)

STEP 1
I was just asked to say a few words about Eric and his reputation as a great campus leader.

STEP 2
Although I didn't have time to prepare a formal speech, it's okay ... because when I think of Eric and the work he has done for this university, two words come to my mind: tenacity and loyalty.

STEP 3
Eric works diligently to get campus programs that all students can enjoy. Many past student leaders promoted their own interests or the interests of their friends ... but not Eric. He makes sure he asks organization leaders what their members want for entertainment and campus improvements.

Connecting words and phrases: But Eric isn't just a tenacious leader, he genuinely loves this school!

No one cheers louder at the football games than Eric. No one supports the theatre productions more than Eric. No one volunteers for philanthropic endeavors more than Eric.

STEP 4

Many have come and gone but no student has done more for this university than Eric. He's a tenacious man. No one shows love for this institution as much as Eric. He's a loyal man.

No one deserves this award more than Eric Kingsley. He's a great student, a great leader . . . a great man.

 ## SOME TIPS FOR FORUMS

Forums are public question and answer sessions. Most forums bring anxiety to those who are subjected to them. No one wants to look silly in front of a lot of people and the fear of not knowing an answer to a question is stressful for many. However, if you remember that you are in front of people who think you have something important to share, and if you remember that there is no crime in not knowing an answer, then you will take some pressure off yourself.

If you are in a speaking situation, you must know something. Chances are, you even know more than most audience members. Therefore, all you have to do is answer their questions to the best of your ability.

If you don't know a specific answer:

- Let the person know you will investigate

- Take his or her phone number or email address

- Respond in a timely manner thus establishing credibility

I've heard people say that they find a speaker MORE credible even though they did not know an answer because that person took the time to find out the answer. It will show that not only are you knowledgeable about some things, but you have character and genuine concern for your audience.

Overall, a presentation with or without a forum, can be amazing if time and effort are put into making it an informative/persuasive, exciting, and wonderful revelation of who you are!

Image © AVAVA, 2009. Used under license from Shutterstock, Inc.

Index

body, of manuscript outline (*continued*)
  for promotion, 100
  for proposals, 116–117
  for religious service, 118–119
  for report of research findings, 122–123
  for response, 149
  for sales pitch, 135–136
  for strategic planning meeting, 94–95
  for team symposium, 138–139
  for toasts, 141–142
  for tours, 144–145
  for tributes, 147
  for welcome, 148
  for workshop/seminars, 151–152
brainstorming, 5
bullet points, in presentation outline, 18

C

call to act, 13
case studies, 25, 124–127
cause and effect, 24
charts, 34
  for sales pitch, 134
chronological order, 24
  in demonstrations, *55*
closure. *See* creative closure
clothing
  for distance communication, 58
  for eulogies, 62
  for fundraising/charity address, 68
  for interviews, 78–79
  for master or mistress of ceremonies, 85
Coleman, Jennifer R., 92–95
colors, 35
comfort, 3
conclusion, of manuscript outline, 11–14
  for announcements, 43, 45
  for award or gift presentation, 110
  for case studies, 126
  for debates, 48, 50
  for dedications, 54
  for demonstrations, 57
  for distance communications, 61
  emotion in, 13
  for eulogies, 64

  for farewells, 66
  for fundraising/charity address, 70–71
  for holiday celebrations, 73
  for informative lectures, 76–77
  intrigue in, 13
  for introduction of keynote speaker, 85
  for master or mistress of ceremonies,
    87–88
  for new job, 100
  for panel discussions, 104
  for persuasive keynote address, 108
  in presentation outline, 20–21
  for promotion, 100
  for proposals, 117
  questions in, 12
  quotations in, 13
  for religious service, 118–119
  for report of research findings, 123–124
  for response, 149
  for sales pitch, 136
  for strategic planning meeting, 95
  for team symposium, 139–140
  for toasts, 142
  for tours, 145
  for tributes, 147
  for welcome, 148–149
  for workshop/seminars, 152
connecting words and phrases, 17–18
  for announcements, 44–45
  for award or gift presentation, 110
  for case studies, 125–126
  for debates, 47–48, 49–50
  for dedications, 54
  for demonstrations, 56
  for distance communications, 60–61
  for eulogies, 63
  for farewells, 65–66
  for fundraising/charity address, 69–70
  for holiday celebrations, 72–73
  for informative lectures, 75–76
  for introduction of keynote speaker, 84
  for persuasive keynote address, 107
  for proposals, 115
  for religious service, 118–119
  for report of research findings, 122–123

qualifications of speaker (*continued*)

    for sales pitch, 135

    for toasts, 141

    for tours, 143

    for tributes, 146

questionnaires, 2

questions

    in conclusion, 12

    in interviews, 82–83

    in introduction, 9

    for panel discussions, 101

    for proposals, 115

    for tours, 145

quotations

    for award or gift presentation, 109

    in conclusion, 13

    for distance communications, 61

    for farewells, 65

    for holiday celebrations, 72, 73

    for informative lectures, 77

    for master or mistress of ceremonies, 88

    for proposals, 117

    for report of research findings, 121

    for strategic planning meeting, 93

    for toasts, 142

    for tours, 143

R

radio. *See* distance communication

refer back, 13

    for demonstrations, 57

    for report of research findings, 124

    for sales pitch, 136

    for strategic planning meeting, 95

rehearsal. *See* practice

relaxation, 6

religious service, 117–119

report of research findings, 120–127

research, for fundraising/charity address, 67

research findings, report of, 120–127

response, 147–149

rhetorical questions, 9, 12

    for demonstrations, 55

    for master or mistress of ceremonies, 86

    for tours, 145

    for workshop/seminars, 152

roastee, 129

roasters, 129

roastmaster, 128

roasts, 127–133

S

sales pitch, 133–136

seating, 3

    for proposals, 114

seminars, 150–152

sensitivity, for roasts, 130

Smith, Tyler, *15, 48,* 137

source citations, 27

statistics, 25

storytelling, 17

strategic planning meetings, 92–95

summer, 4

support, 25–27

T

team symposium, 137–140

    panel discussions and, 137

technical data, 34

television. *See* distance communication

temperature, 3

testimonies, 25

thank you letter, for interviews, 83

things, 4–6

Thompson, Elana Kornegay, 89, 91–92

time, 3

    of eulogies, 62

    limits to, 4, 130

    for meetings, 90

    for persuasive keynote address, 105

    for roasts, 128, 130

    for sales pitch, 134

toasts, 140–142

topics, 4–5

    for award or gift presentation, 109

    for farewells, 65

    for fundraising/charity address, 67, 69

    for holiday celebrations, 72